Habit S

LEAD FROM THE FUTURE

It's Time To Remove The
Habits That Keep You From
The Future Of Your Dreams

Natalie Parks

Table of Contents

Chapter 1:

8 Habits That Can Kill You

Toxic habits in our lives which when left unchecked can lead us to an early grave. We may not be aware of it but it is most definitely eating away at us slowly; like a frog gradually boiling to his death. These invisible yet harmful habits will start appearing in your life if you don't start taking note of it.

Here are 8 habits that can kill you if you're not careful:

1. Being a workaholic.

Man shall eat from the sweat of his brows. Our income pays our bills and puts food on the table. This infers that work is good for it is the backbone on which our survival is pegged upon. It is however not a license to bite more than you can chew. Drowning yourself at work is dangerous for your health.

There is a breaking point for every person. Workaholism is a habit that depressed people do to drown their misery. With only so much that you can handle, you will lose touch with the world if you work without a break. Workaholics are not hard workers who work to make ends meet. They are obsessed with work so that they can forget their problems.

If you are a workaholic who uses business to distract you from your problems, you run the risk of sinking to depression. Take note if stress disorders or suicidal thoughts start to appear. It may be time to seek help to deal with your problems head on instead of masking them in busyness.

2. Isolating yourself from others.

Withdrawal is a red flag any day, anytime. The moment you begin finding comfort in solitude, not wanting to associate with anyone, a problem is in the offing. However, there are times when you will need time alone to meditate and seek peace within yourself.

It is during withdrawal that suicidal thoughts are entertained and sometimes executed. When one isolates themselves from the rest of the world, he becomes blind and deaf to the reality on the ground. You seemingly live in a separate world often mistaken as one of tranquility and peace.

To fight isolation, always find a reason to be around people you share common interests with. It could be sports, writing, acting, or watching. This will help keep off loneliness.

3. Drug and substance abuse.

Drug abuse is a pitfall that many youths have fallen into. It will lead you to an early grave if you do not stop early enough. Apart from the long-term side effects on the health of addicts, drug abuse rips addicts off morality. Most of them become truants, finding themselves on the wrong side of the law and society.

Among the many reasons drug addicts give for drug abuse is that drugs give solace from the harsh world, some kind of temporary blissful haven which the soul longs for. It is unjustifiable to enter into such a health-damaging dungeon to contract respiratory diseases, liver disease, kidney damage, and cardiovascular diseases.

Be careful if you seek drugs as a way to escape from your troubles. If you look closely, most of these people do not end up in a good place after abusing these substances. Seek a healthier alternative instead to let off steam instead.

4. Judging yourself by the standards of others.

As Albert Einstein rightly put it; if we judge a fish by its ability to climb a tree, it will live its whole life believing it is stupid. It is erroneous to use other people's measurement of success to judge your own. This is not to say that you should not be appreciating the achievements of others, but as you do so, give yourself time and space for growth.

The pressure that comes with conforming to your peers' standards can push you down a dark path. Society can be so unforgiving for the faint-hearted. Once you are inside the dark hole of hopelessness, the air of gloom hangs over your head and it can lead you to an early grave. Everyone will forsake you when you fail even after trying to be like them.

5. Being in the wrong company.

Bad company ruins good morals. This truth is as old as civilization. It is not rocket science on how powerful the power of influence from friends is. When in the wrong company, you will be tagged into all sorts of activities they do. Isn't that a direct ticket to hades?

When you lose the power to say No and defend your integrity, morals, and everything that you believe in, then all hell will break loose on you. You would have handed your hypocrite friends the license to ruin your life. Not only will the wrong company ruin your life but also assassinate your character. Keep safe by fleeing from the wrong company when you can before it is too late.

6. Lying.

It looks simple but what many people do not consider is the effect of character assassination caused by a simple lie. Lying makes you unreliable. One client or employer will tell another one and before you know it no one wants anything to do with you.

It may not physically kill you but it will have the power to close all possible open doors of opportunities. Why not be genuine in your dealings and win the trust of your employers and clients? You should jealously protect your reputation because any assault at it is a direct attack on your integrity.

7. Lack of physical exercise.

A healthy body is a healthy mind. To increase your longevity, you need to have a healthy lifestyle. It is not always about the posh vehicle you are driving or the classy estate you live in. How physically fit you are plays a big role in determining your productivity.

You need to walk out there in the sun, go for a morning run, lift weights, do yoga and kegel exercises, or go swimming. Your body needs to be maintained by exercise and not dieting alone. It seems ignoble to be a field person but its benefits are immense.

8. Poor nutritional habits.

The risks of poor nutrition are uncountable. Overeating and obesity come from these habits. Few people pay attention to what they eat, ignorant of the consequences that follow.

Malnutrition and obesity are opposites but stemming from one source – poor nutrition. The eminent danger can no longer be ignored.

According to statistics from the World Health Organization, worldwide obesity has nearly tripled since 1975. In 2016 alone, more than 1.9 billion adults were overweight. The world health body acknowledges that the developmental, economic, social, and medical impacts of the global burden of malnutrition are serious and lasting, for individuals and their families, communities, and countries.

This has come as a shocker to us but it would not have been so if people paid attention to their nutrition habits.

All these 8 habits that can kill you are avoidable if caution is taken. The ball is in your court. Consider carefully whether you want to make a conscious decision to take responsibility and eliminate these damaging habits. You have the power to change if you believe in yourself.

Chapter 2:

8 Habits You Should Have For Life

The key to being happy, feeling energized, and having a productive life relies on a cycle of good habits. Achieving a state of spiritual and physical satisfaction is a conscious choice that you can make for yourself. Realize what attaining the greatest happiness means for you and strive to be as productive as you can to achieve that happiness. Work towards a sense of self-realization and start reaching for your goals one step at a time. Accomplishing this requires you to be confident and have a sense of self, built entirely on good habits. This includes having good attitudes, thoughts, and decision-making skills. Quoting the all-time favorite Poet-Maya Angelou, "a good life is achieved by liking who you are, what you do, and how you do it."

How do you put this in place? Living by good habits and discipline nourishes your potential and make you a better person in your surroundings.

Here are 8 habits you should adopt for life:

1. Create a clear Morning Routine That Is Non-Negotiable

Creating a morning routine that you like and living up to it is essential. Before you start your day, you can turn to what you like doing be it running, meditating, or having a peaceful meal-time at breakfast. Whatever activities you choose based on your liking, kick start your day with that habit. Managing your morning routine and making it a habit enables you to start your day on a proactive and positive note. This will also help you in enhancing your mental health and productivity. Through trial and error find out what works best for you and stick to you day in and out.

2. Make a Point of Physically Exercising Your Body Muscles

To jog your cognitive skills, relieve stress that has a hold on your performance stamina means that you need to exercise-go to the gym regularly or as much as you can. Do you still need more convincing reasons for hitting the gym? Here you go! Physical exercises increase your 'happy' moods chemically and propels the release of hormone endorphins. This hormone aids in getting rid of all the body and mind anxious feelings, hence enabling you to calm down.

3. Develop Quality Personal Relationships With Loved Ones

The Harvard study of adult development has found that most of the existing long-term happiness for an individual is predicted through healthy relationships. Developing and maintaining close relationships with your loved ones or those close to people you consider family has been found to help someone live a longer and quality life. Hence it is the connections within your surroundings that make your life worthwhile.

4. Master an Attitude of Listening

If you want to cultivate relationships in your life, be it professional or personal, communication is key. While communicating with your peers, family, or colleagues, you need to understand that listening to what they are saying is important. This is because you cannot have effective communication if it's one-sided. Remember that it is always important to value what others have to say. Their perspective might impact you, but most importantly, when you listen, you make others feel valued. Always try to understand the other party's point of view even if it defers from yours. Be open-minded to differing opinions. The more you listen, the more you get to learn.

5. Choose Natural Food Rather Than Processed Ones To Help Keep Your Brain Intact.

Whatever we eat always impacts our health, energy, moods, and concentration level. Whether you have weight issues or not, eating a healthy diet is essential. First off, the normality of having a healthy breakfast, lunch, or dinner is an act of practicing self-esteem and self-love. Therefore, eating healthy will always boost your self-esteem, lessen emotional issues, and your daily productivity will eventually be taken care of. If you choose to put unhealthy food in your body, you are not protecting the sanctuary that is giving you life. Make a conscious effort tot choose foods that give you the best chance of success, health, and wellness. As we all know, money can't buy health.

6. Be Appreciative More Than You Are Disparaging

Mastering the art of gratitude is a great way to live a happy, stress-free, healthy, and fulfilling life. As French writer Alphonse said: "We can complain because rose plants have thorns or we can rejoice as thorns also have roses." It's always easy to forget how fortunate you are while trying to push through life and the obstacles that come along with it. How do you master this art? Start a journal of appreciation to be grateful for the things you have. Take the time to appreciate those closest to you, those who care about you, and remember at least one good thing about yourself each and every day. Don't forget to make a note of what you have accomplished as well before you go to bed. The more you take notice of the little joys in life, the happier you will be.

7. Be With a Circle of Friends That Are Positive Minded.

Be careful about who you spend your precious time and energy with. A happy life can be contagious if we know where to attract it. Coincidentally, happiness is also the easiest way to develop positivity in our lives. With that in mind, choose to surround yourself which such people who will bring light into your world. Spend time with those who will nurture you each step of the way and don't hesitate to let go of the people who are eating away at your energy and spirits. Let's not forget the wise words of entrepreneur Jim Rohn, "You are the five people you spent the most time averagely. You only live once! Let it be worthwhile.

8. Take Breaks Regularly To Invest in Self-Care.

Although you might be very passionate about your work and your daily schedules, it is okay to take some time - an hour, minute, second, or even a day off. If you take a while to unwind, you will do wonderful things for your mood, mind, and self-esteem. Spend some time doing at least one thing that makes you feel good every day – whether it be listening to music, engaging in sports, starting a new hobby, dabbling in the arts, or even simply preparing a pleasant meal for yourself, you deserve to do it. Whatever floats your boat, don't neglect it!

Conclusion

Determination, persistence, and continuous effort are essential for the development of these habits. It can take just a few weeks or maybe more than a year to develop your habits, so long as you don't stop. It does not matter how long it takes.

What are you waiting for? Pull up your socks; it's your time to win at life.

Chapter 3:

<u>Five Habits For A Beautiful Life</u>

A beautiful life means different things to different people. However, there are some things that we can all agree about. It is a happy one. Some of us have chased this kind of life but it has proven elusive to the brink of throwing in the towel. We play a greater role in designing a beautiful life for ourselves than others do in our lives.

Here are five habits for a beautiful life:

1. Live The Moment

This is not a call to carelessness. The focal point is to cherish the present moment. We are often distracted by our past experiences even in times when we ought to celebrate our current wins. The present is beautiful because we can influence it.

A beautiful life is joyous and the envy of those who cannot experience it. Savor the present completely and do not be entangled in the past. The past will withhold you from leveraging the opportunities popping up presently. Every saint has a past and every sinner has a future. You can shape the future by living in the moment and not dwelling in the past.

Worrying about the future is not beneficial. If you can change a situation, why worry? If you cannot also change anything, why worry? It is pointless to take the burden of occurrences that are yet to happen. Enjoy your present successes while you can and lead the beautiful life you have been dreaming of.

2.   Plan Wisely

Like everything invaluable, a beautiful life should be planned for. Planning is an integral part of determining whether a beautiful flawless life is achievable or not. It is not an event but a process that requires meticulous attention.

Planning entails extensive allocation of resources to life priorities. You should get your priorities right for things to run smoothly. In planning, your judgment and conscience should be as clear as a cloudless night. Any conflict of interest that could arise will jeopardize the attainment of a beautiful life - the ultimate goal.

We may be forced to make some painful sacrifices along the way and possibly give up short-time pleasures for long-term comfort. It may bring some discomfort but is worth the attainment of a beautiful life. Planning is a heavy price that must be made a routine to anyone aspiring to this magnificent dream.

3.   Pursue Your Purpose

Your purpose is the sole reason that keeps you going in life. You should pursue what motivates you to keep chasing your dreams. A beautiful life is one of fulfillment. Your purpose will bring it effortlessly if you remain loyal to it.

Focusing on your purpose can be a daunting task to an undisciplined mind. Many distractions may come up to make you stray or shift goalposts. You need to be disciplined to continue treading in the narrow path of your purpose. Do not lose sight of the antelope (a beautiful life) because of a dashing squirrel (distractions).

Living a life of purpose will satisfy you because you will willfully do what brings you joy; not what circumstances have forced you to. A cheerful way to live each day like it is your last is by finding pleasure in your routine activities and by extension, your purpose. Pursue it boldly!

4.   Cut Your Coat According To Your Cloth

Live within your means and cut on unnecessary costs. Many people struggle to live within a particular social class that they are not able to afford at the moment. In the process of fitting in, they incur unmanageable debt.

A beautiful life does not mean one of luxury. It is stress-free and affordable within your space. It is unimaginable that one will wear himself/herself out to live a lifestyle beyond reach. Societal pressure should not push you to the brink of self-destruction as you try to fit in other people's shoes.

Even as you work towards your goals, do not suffocate yourself to please other people. Accept your financial status and make your budget within it. You will have an authentic and beautiful life.

5.   Share Your Life With Your Loved Ones

We all have our families and loved ones. Our parents, siblings, spouses, and children should share our lives with us. It is beautiful and desirable that we intertwin our social and personal lives. The warmth and love of our families will put a smile on our faces despite any challenges.

Often, our families are the backbone of our emotional support. We retreat to them when we are wounded by the struggles of life and they nurse us back to health. Their presence and contribution to our lives are immeasurable. Family does not necessarily mean you have to be related by blood.

Some people are strong pillars in our lives and have seen us through hard times. Over time, they have become part of our family. We should share our lives with them and treasure each moment. We would be building a beautiful life for ourselves and the upcoming generations.

These are five habits we need to develop for a beautiful life. We only live once and should enjoy our lifetime by all means.

Chapter 4:

Seven Habits That Will Make You Successful

A man's habits are as good as his lifestyle. Some habits are akin to successful people. The path to greatness is less traveled and the habits to success may be difficult for some people to sustain.

The road to success is narrow and occasionally thorny because habits that will make you successful are uncomfortable and difficult to adapt. Similar to Charles Darwin's theory of survival for the fittest, only those who manage to trim their excesses and shape their habits will eventually be successful.

Here are seven habits that will make you successful:

1. Integrity

Integrity is one of the measures of success. It is the ability to live an honest life free from swindling, blackmail, and corruption among other vices. Integrity is the morality of a person and is relative from one person to another. However, there is a generally accepted threshold of integrity expected of people in different social, political, and economic classes.

Integrity is uncommon to most people making it highly valuable. People will forget how you looked but will never forget how you made them feel. Integrity holds back one from committing such awful mistakes. It will help you award the deserving, condemn vices, be intolerable to corruption, and make transparency your middle name.

The lack of integrity is responsible for the downfall of great people and business empires. Political leaders worldwide have lost their crown of glory to corruption. They were once the dream of every pupil in school and aspiring young leaders looked up to them. Corruption and greed stole that from them.

So powerful is integrity that successful people guard theirs' tooth and nail. Once eroded, their success is at stake. It may crumble down like a mound hill. Do you want to be successful? Have integrity.

2. An Open Mind

It is the ability to tolerate and be receptive to divergent ideas different from your beliefs. It takes a lot to accommodate the opinions of others and accept their reasoning to be rational. Successful people fully understand that they do not have a monopoly on brilliant ideas. As such, they cautiously welcome the proposals of other people while allowing room for further advancement.

Entertaining the ideas of other people does not mean blindly accepting them. It is the habit of successful people to be critical of everything, balancing their options and only settling for the best. An open mind translates to an analytical and inquisitive nature. The zeal to venture into the unknown and experiment with new waters.

Successful people are distinguished from others because they challenge the status quo. They seek to improve their best and develop alternatives to the existing routines. The reason why they are successful in the first place is their open mind.

How does one have an open mind? It is by being open to infinite possibilities of a hundred and one ways of approaching issues. Routine is an enemy of open-mindedness and by extension, success. It is of course inevitable not to follow a routine at our places of work, schools, or families. It is acceptable to that extent. Being its slave is completely unacceptable.

3. Move With Time

Time is never stagnant. The world evolves around time and seasons. The wise is he who deciphers and interprets them correctly. The measure of success in these modern times is different from those in the ancient days. A lot has changed.

In this era of technological advancements, we cannot afford to live in analog ways. The poor readers of seasons are stagnant in one position for a long time. Success is elusive in their hands. A look at business giants will reveal their mastery of times and seasons. They do not fumble at it. Not one bit.

Successful businesses deal with tools of the trade of the modern world. From the great Microsoft corporation to the Coca-cola company. All of them align themselves with the market demand presently. Learning the present time and season is a habit that will elevate you to success.

4. Learn From The Mistakes of Others

It is prudent to learn from the mistakes of other people and not from yours. Keenly observe those ahead of you and watch out not to fall into their traps. It is regretful to be unable to take a cue from our predecessors and learn from their failures.

Successful people travel down roads once taken (for the advantage of hindsight) by others – except for a few adventurous ones who venture into the unknown. The benefit of hindsight is very important because we learn from the mistakes of those who preceded us and adjust accordingly. Develop a habit of watching closely those ahead of you and take a cue from them not to commit similar mistakes. This habit will propel you to the doorstep of success.

5. Investment Culture

It is prudent to be mindful of tomorrow. No amount of investment is too little. Successful people do not consume everything they produce. They save a portion of their income for the future. Investment is a culture developed over time. Some people find it difficult to postpone the entire consumption of their income. They will only settle when nothing is left. This is retrogressive.

An investment culture curbs wastage and emphasizes tomorrow's welfare. Moreover, to reduce risk, the investment portfolio is diversified. It is dangerous to risk everything in one endeavor. Captains of industries worldwide have invested broadly in different sectors. This makes them stay afloat even during tough economic seasons.

6. Choosing Your Battles

On your way to success, do not make many enemies. This habit is ancient but very relevant to date. Unnecessary fights will wear you out and divert you away from the goal. Petty distractions will hijack your focus and successfully make you unsuccessful.

Learn to train your guns on things that matter. Feed your focus and starve your fears. Ignore useless petty issues that may lead to tainting of your public image. Fight your battles wisely.

7. Learn To Listen

Listening is an art beyond hearing. It is paying detailed attention to the speech of others, both verbal and non-verbal. Always listen more and talk less – a common argument for having two ears and one mouth. To be successful, you will have to pay closer attention to what is unspoken. Listen to the way people communicate. You will pick up genuine intentions in their speech and align yourself accordingly.

Once perfected, these seven habits will make you successful.

Chapter 5:

Make Friends With Your Problems

Today we're going to talk about a topic that I hope will inspire you to view your problems not as a hurdle to your goals, but a necessity. How you can make friends with your problems to eventually see it as a part of your journey towards greater success.

You see, problems arise in all aspects of our lives every single day. As we go through life, we start to realise that life is merely about problem solving. When we are growing up, we face the problems of not being able to stand on our own two feet, problems about not being able to potty train, problems with peeing in the bed, problems with riding a new bicycle, problems with school, problems with Teachers, problems with our homework.

But the thing is that as kids, we view these problems as challenges. As something to work towards. We don't necessarily view problems as a negative thing, and we always strive to overcome these problems, never giving up until we do so. And through this perseverance, we grow and evolve. But as we get older, and our child-like response to problems start to change, we start seeing problems in a different way. Problems become obstacles rather than challenges, and problems sometimes overwhelm us to the point where we are not able to function.

We face problems in getting into good high schools and universities, problems in getting a job, problems with family, problems with relationships, problems with bosses, problems with colleagues, problems with starting a family. All these are legitimate problems that I am very sure every single one of us will face at some point in our lives. And the problems will never stop coming.

From what I have shared so far, it is very clear that problems are a way of life, and problems will never go away. A life without problems is really not life at all.

Personally, I have dealt with my fair share of problems. I struggled greatly with getting good grades in university, I struggled in serving for the army as part of mandatory conscription for my country, I struggled with pressures from work, and these problems at times got to me where I felt that I could not see the light at the end of the tunnel. These problems consumed my vision that I could not see the big picture. That life is beautiful, and that my problems are nothing compared to what life has to offer.

In that moment as I was living through those problems however, I could not see the light. I was laser focused on the problem at hand and at many stages, I did feel depressed. I felt unworthy. I felt like I couldn't handle my problems.

I am not sure if my inability to handle problems as I grew older were genetic, or that my character just wasn't strong enough to withstand pressures from the external world. But I did feel like it became harder and harder each year.

What I failed to realise, and that goes back to how I saw problems when I was young, was that I viewed my problems as an enemy rather than a friend. I saw my problems as something that was getting in the way of my goals, rather than a necessary part of the process towards that goal.

By the time I was 20, I wanted a life without problems. I didn't want to deal with any more problems anymore. And as unrealistic as that sounded, I actually believed that it was what I wanted. And every problem that came my way felt like a mountain. A major annoyance that would take every ounce of my energy to overcome. And that negative view to problems actually made my life much more miserable.

It was only in my late twenties that I saw more of life did my perception of problems start to shift profoundly. I learned of the struggles that my parents had to go through to get the life that I was living today, I saw in many of my peers that work life is actually tough and those that viewed their job negatively almost always ended up depressed and unworthy while those that saw their work as challenges actually grew as people.

That shift happened gradually but I started to see the problems that came up in my daily life as friends rather than as enemies. I started to view the mandatory things I had to do to sustain myself financially, emotionally, physically, as simply a way of life. In areas such as health and fitness where I tend to struggle with a lot, which was quite a big problem in my opinion, i simply found alternative ways to keep fit that worked for me rather than get obsessed with the way i looked.

In areas of finance and career, where I also saw as a big problem, I adapted by adopting a completely novel way of working that actually made my work much more meaningful and enjoyable instead of subscribing myself to a job that I know that I would hate.

I started to view each problem as challenges again that would require my knowledge and expertise to overcome. And it started to consume me less and less. I made them my friends instead of my enemy. And when one door closes, I was always resourceful to find another open door to get me to where I wanted to go.

So I challenge each and everyone of you to start seeing your problems not as hindrances to your goals, but as challenges that requires your smartness to conquer. I believe that you have the power to knock down every problem that comes your way no matter how great the challenge is. However if it does become overwhelming, it is okay to walk away from it. Don't let it consume you and don't obsess over a problem until it wrecks your health mentally and physically. Life is too short for problems to ruin us. If it can't be made friends with, it is okay to simply let it go. Nothing good can come from sheer force.

Chapter 6:

6 Habits of Oprah Winfrey

When anyone utters the name "Oprah Winfrey," one of her most iconic quotes comes to mind: "You get a car, and everyone else gets a car." While most business people applaud the "to-do roster," Oprah is not one of them; instead, she values meditation, no alarms, and limiting business operations to the necessary minimum. From a poor rural Mississippi upbringing to getting a full scholarship and to landing a seat on the morning talk program, Baltimore Is Talking, to now solidifying her reputation as a global legend and America's first black billionaire, with a net worth of US$2.5 billion, you might be wondering – exactly how she does it?

Oprah Winfrey maintains a series of daily routines-from getting up early to work out to practicing Gratitude. This daily routine, as she notes, keeps her happy, grounded, and humble.

Here are six daily habits from the legend herself that you might want to make your own.

1. Her Day Starts With Morning Rituals.

Oprah Winfrey starts her mornings with a sequence of spiritual exercises, allowing her body to wake up and her mind to focus on Gratitude and self-reflection. She meditates for approximately 20 minutes. If the weather is nice, she sits in her lawn chair with her eyes closed, simply reminiscing on the previous day and imagining her aspirations for the day ahead. She noted that starting the day slowly allows her mind to wake up and become entirely focused on the day ahead.

2. Working Out Every Morning

Oprah's journey to weight loss has been a struggle over the years. She opened up on her efforts with maintaining a healthy weight and fitness program. She highlighted in an interview that she loves sweating it up through the regular old-fashioned cardio exercises, explicitly on an elliptical machine followed by a treadmill. She then follows with some regular bodyweight training before warming up for some sit-ups.

Although there is ongoing research on whether a better fitness routine should be in the morning or the evening, substantial studies describe several morning fitness benefits. To mention a few, You'll eat fewer calories; you'll have more energy throughout the day, burn more bothersome fat cells, and sleep better when the sun goes down.

3. She Consumes a Lot of Vegetables

If you don't pay attention when your mother or your partner softly encourages you to eat more of Mother Earth's natural creations, maybe you'll listen to Oprah Winfrey.

Oprah confessed in an interview that she values her lunch more than any other meal, and one of her meals go-to involves a big, overflowing salad of green goodness. She noted that the salad is usually from the veggies from her home garden. As she put its's "as a rule, if we can grow it, we don't buy it."

You probably don't need us to tell you that veggies are excellent for your diet. Still, science backs up Winfrey's meal plan, as a well-balanced, vegetable patch diet can help fight cancer, heart disease, diabetes, and hypertension, among other conditions.

4. Oprah Schedules Time To Unwind

There's no doubt that Winfrey's itinerary would be overwhelming for most people, with regular meetings, phone conversations, and traveling, but achieving this degree of esteem necessitates astute management and perseverance. However, if you look into the lives of individuals at the pinnacle of success, such as Winfrey, you'll notice that they constantly make time to unwind.

In an interview about her daily life, Winfrey stated that she relaxes before retiring to bed by reading frequently. Though you may not have Winfrey's gorgeous fireplace to warm you up as you flip the pages over, the research found that individuals who read before bed are less anxious than those who watch Netflix.

5. Practicing Gratitude daily.

The benefits of practicing Gratitude have been proven for centuries, even though gestures to the same have become popular recently. Oprah maintains with her volumes of gratitude diaries that she usually jots down before going to bed. She makes a list of things that have given her tremendous joy or which she is grateful for.

Implementing this habit will not only improve your health but also increase your empathy and self-confidence. One study suggests that thinking about what you're thankful for rather than contemplating on the to-do list each night helps better your sleep.

6. She Manages Her Finances.

You'd think someone of Winfrey's caliber would employ someone to manage her finances, but while she got a whole team, she oversees the minutiae of her fortune daily. She claims that she cannot delegate all financial decisions to others because she had a poor upbringing and prefers to understand what comes in and what goes out of her earnings. She noted during an interview that it is crucial for her to personally manage her finances as doing so relieves her from surprises of what she has and doesn't have.

While most of us struggle with the very thought about money, research has shown that the more you train yourself to handle your finances, the better your chances of becoming wealthy.

Conclusion

Just as Oprah, if you are invariably striving to achieve greatness in all life aspects, you must maintain a couple of healthy habits. If Oprah's journey inspires you, then flexing to the above routine might be your thing. Who knows!

Chapter 7:

Keep Working When You're Just Not Feeling It

How many times in a day do you feel like doing nothing? How many times have you had the feeling of getting exhausted and have no energy or motivation to do anything? Do you want answers to these problems? Let's analyze some things.

What were the last big achievement that made you, your family, and your friends proud? When was the last time you had this urge to do a little more work just for the sake of it? Did you feel sorry for yourself and thought how tired you are? These are the problems!

The things that don't make sense to you right now will become more meaningful and purposeful once you get out of your comfort zone. For that, you must start doing what you failed to do the last time.

These feelings of in-activeness and leisure are not a result of some circumstances but the inner voice of every human being that never sleeps and makes us feel like we cannot do this today.

More than often, a change of self is needed than a change of the scenes surrounding us. This is the major task at hand that most people fail to achieve. But we can never give up. This is in fact the spirit of living. The spirit of keep going even when the hardest times hit.

Your body should be the easiest item for you to train and get a hold of. If you are not even able to do that, then there is very little hope for you to achieve anything ever again.

So put yourself in motion and start creating. Instead of thinking about these wrong feelings that your heart gives out just to get you to sleep one more hour, use your time to get creative with life. You don't deserve a good sleep if you haven't done what was meant to be done today. You don't deserve a long breath of relaxation if you haven't tried hard enough to get out of this rut.

You don't feel like getting the job done because you still have a sense of fear and self-pity that keeps you from giving your creative energies another try.

Human beings are the summary of what they repeatedly do, so excellence can also be a habit once you make changes in your behavior for it.

If an inner voice tells you not to do something because you cannot do it, give it a trailer of what is about to come. You will get things done the very first time, and that voice will never bother you again.

These voices and feelings will make you procrastinate rather than performing those actions for real. This is no good way to use your creative energies, just to think of a beautiful scenario and not actually doing something to be in that scenario someday. And laying low because you don't feel like doing it today is the smallest hurdle to pass to get to that place.

All you need is some self-resilience and self-control and the ability to be the master of your body and I doubt there is anything that can stop you then.

Chapter 8:

How To Achieve True Happiness

How many of us actually know what happiness really is? And how many of us spend our whole lives searching for it but never seem to be happy?

I want to share with you my story today of how i stumbled upon true happiness and how you can achieve the same for yourself in your life.

Many of us go through the motion of trying to earn money because we think the more money we have, the better our lives will be. We chase the dream of increasing our earning power so that we can afford to buy nicer and more expensive things. And we believe that when we have more money, our happiness level will increase as well and we will be filled with so much money and happiness that we can finally stop chasing it.

Now I just wanna say, Yes, for those who come from a not so affluent background where they have a family to feed and basic needs have to be met to in order for them to survive, having a monetary goal to work towards is truly commendable as their drive, motivation, and sole purpose comes from supporting their family. Their sense of achievement, joy, and happiness comes from seeing their loved ones attaining basic needs and then go on to achieve success later in life at the expense of their time and energy. But they are more than okay with that and they do so with a willing heart, mind, and soul. You might even say that these people have achieved true happiness. Not because they are chasing more money, but because they are using that money to serve a greater purpose other than themselves.

But what about the rest of us who seemingly have everything we could ever want but never seem to be happy? We work hard at our jobs every single day waiting for our next promotion so that we can command a higher pay. And as our income grows, so does our appetite and desire for more expensive material things.

For guys we might chase that fancy new watch like rolex, omega, breitling, drooling over that model that always seem to be on a never-ending waitlist. And as we purchased one, feeling that temporary joy and satisfaction, we quickly look towards that next model as the shiny object we have starts to slowly fade. We lose our so-called happiness in time and We go back to work dreaming about that next watch just to feel that joy and excitement again. This could apply to other material things such as a shiny new technology gadgets smartphones, tv, and even cars.

For women, while might not be true for everyone, They might look towards that designer shoe, that branded handbag, ar that fancy jewellery that costs thousands of dollars to purchase but happily pay for it because they think it makes them feel better about ourselves. Or they could even use these purchases as retail therapy from their stressful lives and jobs.

Whatever these expensive purchases may be, we think that by spend our hard earned money on material things, it will bring us happiness and joy, but somehow it never does, and in most cases it is only temporary satisfactions.

That was exactly what happened with me. I kept chasing a higher income thinking it would bring me happiness. As a lover of technology, I always sought to buy the latest gadgets I could get my hands on. The excitement peaks and then fades. For me I realised that I had created an endless loop of trying to chase happiness but always coming up short.

One day I sat down and reflected on what exactly made me REALLY happy and I started writing down a list.

My List Came down to these in no particular order: Spending time with family, spending time with friends, helping others, having a purpose in life, being at peace with myself, working on my own dreams, singing and making music, exercising, being grateful, and finally being a loving person to others.

As I went through this list, I realised that hey, in none of the list did i write "making more money" or "buying more things". And it finally dawned on me that these are REALLY the things that made me truly happy. And only after I had defined these things did i actively choose to do more of them every single day.

I started spending more quality time with my friends and family, i started playing my favourite sport (Tennis) a few times a week, I chose to be grateful that I can even be alive on this earth, and I chose to be more loving and humble. Finally I also actively chose not to compare myself to people who were more "successful" than I was because comparing yourself to others can NEVER make you happy and will only make you feel inferior when you are not. Always remember that You are special, you are unique, and you are amazing.

After doing these things every single day, I had become a much happier person. It is all about perspective.

So what can you do to achieve happiness for yourself?

I recommend that you do the same thing I did which is to write down a list under the title "When Am I The Happiest?" or "When Was A Time When I Truly Felt Happy?" Start breaking down these memories as you recall your past, and down the essence of the memory. Everybody's list will be different as happiness means different things to every one of us. Once you have your answer, start doing more of these things everyday and tell me how you feel afterwards.

Some days you will forget about what makes you truly happy as you get bombarded by the harsh and cruel things life will throw at you. So I encourage you to put this list somewhere visible where you can see it everyday. Constantly remind yourself of what happiness means to you and shift your mind and body towards these actions every single day. I am sure you will be much happier person after that. See you in the next one :)

Chapter 9:

10 Habits of Emma Stone

Emma Stone, an Academy Award-winning actress made her debut in 2007 with the teen comedy "Superbad." Since then, she has become one of the most demanded actress of her time, amassing honours, nominations and captivating audiences on and off the big screen with her effortless, pleasant acting style and her attitude.

Stone's wide eyes and seemingly effortless brilliance shine through in practically every job she lands, making her one of the most renowned movies star. But, even if you've seen every one of Stone's films, there are likely a few facts you don't know about this extraordinary actress.

Here are 10 habits of Emma Stone that can be yours too.

1. Be Your Worst Judgement

According to Emma Stone, being your worst critique push you to work hard on yourself because your set standards are high. As long as you're true to yourself, what others think is not a concern. It's not about being cruel to oneself but about pushing yourself to new heights.

2. Understand Your Interests

Emma presented a PowerPoint presentation of her work to her parents for review. That earned her permission to relocate to Los Angeles in 2004 to pursue her acting career. She knew exactly what she wanted because it was her passion, and she didn't let anyone get in her way. You know you're enthusiastic about something when you're willing to go to any length to make it happen.

3. A Clear Vision

Stone is always quite clear about what she wants out of life. She does not allow short-term distractions or anything else to get in her way. She feels that the key to success is first to decide exactly what you want. The more precise your concept, the easier it will be to make it come to life.

4. Perseverance

Emma stone's route to Success, for example, her character Mia in La La La Land, was never an easy one. After she moved to California, she tried several roles, which was until 2007 she gained widespread notoriety for her appearance in the comedy "Superbad."

It took her five years have her first taste of success in acting. That kind of perseverance keeps her striving for the best, and so can you.

5. Education Equates No Worth

Stone has didn't allow societal assumptions and stigma to limit her. She made her acting debut when she was 11 years old. At the age of 15, she decided to drop out of high school and to pursue her acting career. In a world full of standardized tests, it is normal for people to assess you based on your educational level or even link it to your level of Success.

6. Eat that Dang Red Velvet Cupcake

The world is your oyster, and life is brief. So live your life, and don't allow anything to stop you from making the most of it.

7. No Barriers You Can't Conquer

Emma Stone revealed that she suffered from anxiety and panic attacks as a child. She opted for treatment and performance to help her get over it and keep chasing her aspirations. When you face challenges in your life, giving up is like giving up on the critical part of yourself. Losing faith in yourself means that your aspirations and passions are put on hold.

8. Do What Brings You Joy

If you are dissatisfied with your current circumstances, you must make a change. Life is too short to spend it doing things that make you miserable or even melancholy. For Emma, this means that you should treat yourself now and then, especially on bad days. Cherish the little things in life.

9. Look Up to Your Role Models

Emma broke down in tears when Mel B spoke to her through a video message. Of course, you don't have to cry when you meet your role model. But it's magnificent to have someone to look up to, that strong person who gives you strength on bad days.

10. Don't Over Plan

Having a precise aim and knowing where you want to go in life is absolutely a positive thing. But don't over plan because life might take an unexpected turn at any time. Emma, in an interview, said that she is a person who will never make a five-year plan and that she only depends on her intuition. Follow your intuition, and if it's correct, things will fall into place.

Conclusion

As Emma did, live your life, and don't allow anything to stop you from making the most of it.

Chapter 10:

Why You're Demotivated By A Values Conflict

Every human being, in fact, every organism in this universe is different from even the same member of their species. Every one of us has different traits, likes, dislikes, colors, smells, interests so it's natural to have a difference of opinion.

It's natural to have a different point of view. It's natural and normal to have a different way of understanding. And it's definitely normal for someone else to disagree with your ways of dealing with things.

Most of us don't want to see someone disagreeing with us because we have this tricky little fellow inside of us that we call EGO.

Our ego makes us feel disappointed when we see or hear someone doing or saying something better than us. We cannot let go of the fact that someone might be right or that someone might be Okay with being wrong and we can't do a single thing about it.

This conflict of values occurs within ourselves as well. We want to do one thing but we cannot leave the other thing as well. We want to have something but we cannot keep it just because we don't have the resources to maintain them.

This feeling of 'want to have but cannot have' makes us susceptible to feelings of incompleteness ultimately making us depressed. The reality of life is that you can't always get what you want. But that doesn't make it a good enough reason to give up on your dreams or stop thinking about other things too.

Life has a lot to offer to us. So what if you can't have this one thing you wanted the most. Maybe it wasn't meant for you in the first place. Nature has a way of giving you blessings even when you feel like you have nothing.

Let's say you want something but your mind tells you that you can't have it. So what you should do is to find alternative ways to go around your original process of achieving that thing and wait for new results. What you should do is to give up on the idea altogether just because you have a conflict within your personality.

You cannot let this conflict that is building within you get a hold of you. Clear your mind, remove all doubts, get rid of all your fears of failure or rejection, and start working from a new angle with a new perspective. Set new goals and new gains from the same thing you wanted the first time.

This time you might get it just because you already thought you had nothing to lose.

This feeling of 'No Regret' will eventually help you get over any situation you ever come across after a fight with your inner self. This feeling can help you flourish in any environment no matter what other people say or do behind your back.

Nothing can bring you peace but yourself. Nothing holds you back but your other half within you.

Chapter 11:

Discovering Your Strengths and

Weaknesses

Today we're going to talk about a very simple yet important topic that hopefully brings about some self discovery about who you really are. By the end of this video i wish to help you find out what areas you are weak at so that maybe you could work on those, and what your strengths are so that you can play to them and lean into them more for greater results in your career and life in general.

We should all learn to accept our flaws as much as we embrace our strengths. And we have to remember that each of us are unique and we excel in different areas. Some of us are more artistic, some visionary, some analytical, some hardworking, some lazy, what matters is that we make these qualities work for us in our own special way.

Let's start by identifying your weaknesses. For those of you that have watched enough of my videos, you would know that i encourage all of you to take a pen to write things down. So lets go through this exercise real quick. Think of a few things that people have told you that you needed to work on, be it from your Teachers, your friends, your family, or whoever it may be.

How many of these weaknesses would you rate as significantly important that it would affect your life in a drastic way if you did not rectify it? I want you to put them at the top of your list. Next spend some time to reflect and look in the mirror. Be honest with yourself and identify the areas about yourself that you know needs some work.

Now I want you to take some time to identity your strengths. Repeat the process from above, what are the things people have told you about yourself that highlighted certain qualities about you? Whether that you're very outgoing, friendly, a great singer, a good team player, very diligent. I want you to write as many of these down as you can. No matter how big or small these strengths are, I want you to write down as many as you can.

Now I want you to also place your 3 biggest strengths at the top of the list. As I believe these are the qualities that best represent who you are as a person.

Now that you've got these 2 lists. I want you to compare them. Which list is longer? the one with strengths or weaknesses? If you have more weaknesses, that's okay, it just means that there is more room for improvement. If you have more strengths, thats good.

What we are going to do with this list now is to now make it a mission to improve our weaknesses and play heavily into our strengths for the foreseeable future. You see, our strengths are strengths for a reason, we are simply naturally good at it. Whether it be through genetics, or our personalities, or the way we have been influenced by the world. We should all try to showcase our strengths as much as we can. It is hard for me to say exactly what that is, but I believe that you will know how you maximise the use of your talent. Whether it be serving others, performing for others, or even doing specific focused tasks. Simply do more of it. Put yourself in more situations where you can practice these strengths. And keep building on it. It will take little effort but yield tremendous results.

As for your weaknesses, I want you to spend some time on the top 3 that you have listed so far. As these could be the areas that have been holding you back the most. Making improvements in these areas could be the breakthrough that you need to become a much better person and could see you achieving a greater level success than if you had just left them alone.

I challenge each and everyone of you to continually play to your strengths, sharpening them until they are sharp as a knife, while working on smoothening the rough edges of your weaknesses. So that they may balance out your best qualities.

Chapter 12:

Happy People Engage in Deep Meaningful Conversations

Psychologist Matthias Mehl and his team set out to study happiness and deep talk. In the journal Psychological Science, his study involved college students who wore an electronically activated recorder with a microphone on their shirt collar that captured 30-second snippets of conversation every 12.5 minutes for four days. Effectively, this created a conversational "diary" of their day.

Then researchers went through the conversations and categorized them as either small talk (talk about the weather, a recent TV show, etc.) or more substantive discussion (talk about philosophy, current affairs, etc.). Researchers were careful not to automatically label specific topics a certain way—if the speakers analyzed a TV show's characters and their motivations, this conversation was considered substantive.

The researchers found that about a third of the students' conversations were considered substantive, while a fifth consisted of small talk. Some conversations didn't fit neatly into either category, such as discussions that focused on practical matters like who would take out the trash.

The researchers also studied how happy the participants were, drawing data from life satisfaction reports the students completed and feedback from people in their lives.

The results? Mehl and his team found that the happiest person in the study had twice as many substantive conversations, and only one-third the small talk, as the unhappiest person. Almost every other conversation the happiest person had—about 46 percent of the day's conversations—was substantive.

As for the unhappiest person, only 22 percent of that individual's conversations were substantive, while small talk made up only 10 percent of the happiest person's conversations.

Does small talk equal unhappiness? Score one for Team Introvert because we've known this all along.

How to Have More Meaningful Conversations

instead of

- "How are you?"

- "How was your weekend?"

- "Where did you grow up?"

- "What do you do for a living?"

- "What's your story?"

- "What was your favorite part of your weekend?"

- "Tell me something interesting about where you grew up."

- "What drew you to your line of work?"

Why Is Happiness Linked with Deep Talk?

Further research is still needed because it's not clear whether people make themselves happier by having substantive conversations or whether people who are already happy choose to engage in meaningful talk. However, one thing is evident: Happiness and meaningful interactions go hand-in-hand.

In an interview with the *New York Times*, Mehl discussed the reasons he thinks substantive conversations are linked to happiness. For one, humans are driven to create meaning in their lives, and substantive conversations help us do that, he said. Also, human beings—both introverts and extroverts—are social animals who have a real need to connect with others. Substantive conversation connects, while small talk doesn't.

Chapter 13:
Saying Yes To Things

Today we're going to talk about why saying yes can be a great thing for you and why you should do so especially in social invites.

Life you see is a funny thing. As humans, we tend to see things one dimensionally. And we tend to think that we have a long life ahead of us. We tend to take things for granted. We think we will have time to really have fun and relax after we have retired and so we should spend all our efforts and energy into building a career right now, prioritising it above all else. When faced with a choice between work and play, sometimes many of us, including myself choose work over social invites.

There were periods in my life that i routinely chose work over events that it became such a habit to say no. Especially as an entrepreneur, the interaction between colleagues or being in social events is almost reduced to zero. It became very easy and comfortable to live in this bubble where my one and only priority in life is to work work work. 24 hours, 7 days a week. Of course, in reality a lot of time was wasted on social media and Netflix, but u know, at least i could sort of pretend that i was kind of working all day. And I was sort of being productive and sort of working towards my goals rather than "wasting time on social events". That was what I told myself anyway.

But life does not work that way. As I prioritised work over all else, soon all the social invite offers started drying up. My constant "nos" were becoming evident to my social circle and I was being listed as perpetually unavailable or uninterested in vesting time or energy into any friendships or relationships. And as i retreated deeper and deeper into this black hole of "working remotely" i found myself completely isolated from new experiences and meeting new people, or even completely stopped being involved in any of my friend's lives.

I've successfully written myself out of life and I found myself all alone in it.

Instead of investing time into any meaningful relationships, I found that my closest friends were my laptop, tablet, phone, and television. Technology became my primary way of interacting with the world. And I felt connected, yet empty. I was always plugged in to wifi, but i lived my life through a screen instead of my own two eyes. My work and bedroom became a shell of a home that I spent almost all my time, and life just became sort of pointless. And I just felt very alone.

As I started to feel more and more like something was missing, I couldn't quite make out what it was that led me to this feeling. I simply though to myself, hey I'm prioritising work and my career, making money is what the internet tells me I should do, and not having a life is simply part of the price you have to pay... so why am I so incredibly unhappy?

As it turns out, as I hope many of you have already figured out at this point, that life isn't really just about becoming successful financially.

While buying a house, getting a car, and all that good stuff is definitely something that we should strive towards, we should not do so at the expense of our friends. That instead of saying no to them, we should start saying yes, at least once in a while. We need to signal to our friends that hey, yes even though I'm very busy, but I will make an effort to carve out time for you, so that you know I still value you in my life and that you are still a priority.

We need to show our friends that while Monday may not work for us, that I have an opening maybe 2 weeks later if you're still down. That we are still available to grow this friendship.

I came to a point in my life where I knew something had to change. As I started examining my life and the decisions I had made along the way with regards to my career, I knew that what I did wrong was saying no WAAAAAY too often. As I tried to recall when was the last time I actually when I went out with someone other than my one and only BFF, I simply could not. Of the years that went by, I had either said that I was too busy, or even on the off chances that I actually agreed to some sort of meetup, I had the habit of bailing last minute on lunch and dinner appointments with friends. And I never realized that i had such a terrible reputation of being a flaker until I started doing some serious accounting of my life. I had become someone that I absolutely detested without even realising it. I have had people bail on me at the very last minute before, and I hated that feeling. And whenever someone did that to me, I generally found it difficult to ask them out again because I felt that they weren't really that interested in meeting me anyway. That they didn't even bother to reschedule the appointment. And little did I know, I was becoming that very same person and doing the very thing that I hate to my friends. It is no wonder that I started dropping friends like flies with my terrible actions.

As I came to this revelation, I started panicking. It was as if a truck had hit me so hard that I felt that I was in a terrible accident. That how did I let myself get banged up to that extent?

I started scrolling through my contact lists, trying to find friends that might still want to hang out with me. I realized that my WhatsApp was basically dry as a desert, and my calendar was just work for the last 3 years straight with no meaningful highlights, no social events worth noting.

It was at this point that I knew I had made a huge mistake and I needed to change course immediately. Salvaging friendships and prioritising social activities went to the top of my list.

I started creating a list of friends that I had remotely any connection to in the last 5 years and I started asking them out one by one. Some of my friends who i had asked out may not know this, but at that point in my life, i felt pretty desperate and alone and I hung on to every meeting as if my life depended on it. Whilst I did manage to make some appointments and met up with some of them. I soon realized that the damage had been done. That my friends had clearly moved on without me... they had formed their own friends at work and elsewhere, and I was not at all that important to have anymore. It was too little too late at that point and there was not much I could do about it. While I made multiple attempts to ask people out, I did not receive the same offers from people. It felt clearly like a one-way street and I felt that those people that I used to call friends, didn't really see me as one. You see growing a friendship takes time, sometimes years of consistent meetups before this person becomes indispensable in your life. Sharing unique experiences that allow your friends to see that you are truly vested in them and that you care about them and want to spend time with them. I simply did not give myself that chance to be integrated into someone's life in that same way, I did not invest that time to growing those friendships and I paid the price for it.

But I had to learn all these the hard way first before I can receive all the good that was about to come in the future.

Chapter 14:

Happy People Are Optimistic

Beyond the simple reality that optimists are happier people (and happiness is what you're striving for), optimism has other benefits as well. So, if you want to achieve greater happiness, try being optimistic for a day.

Optimists enjoy a greater degree of academic success than pessimists do. Because optimistic students think it's possible for them to make a good grade, they study hardier and they study smarter. They manage the setting in which they study and they seek help from others when they need it. (Optimism, it turns out, is almost as predictive of how well students do in college as the SAT.)

Optimists are more self-confident than pessimists are. They believe in *themselves* more than fate.

Optimists are more likely to be problem-solvers than pessimists are. When pessimistic students get a D on a test, they tend to think things like: "I knew I shouldn't have taken this course. I'm no good at psychology." The optimistic student who gets a D says to herself, "I can do better. I just didn't study enough for this test. I'll do better next time." And she will.

Optimists welcome second chances after they fail more than pessimists do. Optimistic golfers always take a *mulligan* (a redo swing without penalty). Why? Because they expect to achieve a better result the second time around.

Optimists are more socially outgoing than pessimists are. Socially outgoing folks believe that the time they spend with other human beings makes them better in some way — smarter, more interesting, more attractive. Unfortunately, pessimists see little, if any, benefit from venturing out into the social world.

Optimists are not as lonely as pessimists are. Because pessimists don't see as much benefit from socializing with others, they have far fewer social and emotional connections in their lives, which is what loneliness is all about.

Optimists utilize social support more effectively than pessimists do. They aren't afraid to reach out in times of need.

Optimists are less likely to blame others for their misfortune than pessimists are. When you blame someone else for your troubles, what you're really saying is, "You're the *cause* of my problem and, therefore, you have to be the *solution* as well." Optimists have just as many troubles as pessimists throughout life — they just accept more responsibility for dealing with their misfortune.

Optimists cope with stress better than pessimists do. Pessimists worry, optimists act. A patient with coronary heart disease who is pessimistic "hopes and prays" that he doesn't have another heart attack anytime soon. The optimistic heart patient leaves little to chance — instead, he exercises regularly, practices his meditation exercises, adheres to a low-cholesterol diet, and makes sure he always gets a good night's sleep.

Chapter 15:

How To Be Comfortable With Discomfort

"The cure for pain is in the pain." - Rumi.

We've become so accustomed to living and striving for everyday life that if anything goes against it, our natural reaction is to ease it quickly. This doesn't only go for physical pain. We look for metaphorical medicine even when we feel emotional discomforts such as guilt, shame, or vulnerability. We dive into distractions instead of looking into the deeper causes of our emotional distresses. The avoidance of pain and discomfort has become a way of our lives.

We often mistake pleasure with happiness without knowing that satisfaction is brought to us by external factors while joy comes from within. It depends upon our views and perceptions of situations and people and something we always control. We have to make sure that we don't beat ourselves up with temporary distractions or reach for band-aids to avoid something uncomfortable. Turning distraction into opportunity and bringing yourself back to the present is what we should strive for. We should turn down our speed to a snail's pace because when we do something slower, it enables us to put in touch with our consciousness and physical sensations. It is then that we can dive into identifying the origin of our pain and where it resonates. We should be able to hang out with the hurt so we can begin to heal.

"What you resist, persists." - Carl Jung. The pain and discomfort that we feel act as messengers for us. If we avoid or cover them, they are bound to return. We should listen closely to what our pain is trying to tell us. Our happiness doesn't lie in eliminating painful situations; instead, it is connected to handling and perceiving them. We think that resistance is the only thing that will save us, but resistance is what makes us sink further into the hurt.

Pain hurts, and discomfort returns when we don't sit with them and get to know them. It's impressive to discover that many of our physical discomforts are brought on by our internal hurts like anxiety, stress, and loneliness. Once we recognize the true root of our pain, we can create a plan to heal the actual wound instead of placing metaphorical band-aids on it. It's better to breathe and connect your body to your mind to enforce control over your thoughts. This will help you handle any situation or crisis with betterment the next time it arises.

Chapter 16:

<u>10 Habits of Happy People</u>

Happy people live the most satisfying lives on the planet. They have come to understand the importance of not worrying because it will not make any differential change in their lives. If you cannot control the outcome of a process, why worry? If you can control and make a difference to the outcome of a situation, why worry? Worrying does not bring an ounce of success your way.

Here are 10 habits of happy people that could be you if you choose to adopt it:

1. <u>Happy People Count Their Blessings.</u>

Taking stock of your successes is an important part of appreciating yourself. You find comfort in knowing that despite all the hiccups you have found in your journey there remains an oasis of achievements in your desert.

Everyone needs to take stock of what is in his or her basket of blessings. It is a reminder of your resilience and persistence in the face of challenges. It is an indication of your ability and a minute representation of the progress you can make, given time.

Remind yourself of the taste of victory in your small achievements. It begins with understanding that you definitely cannot be able to win it all. There are grey and shadow areas that will not be within your reach.

2. Happy People Do Not Need the Validation of Others.

Happy people do not wait for the validation of other people. They are autonomous. Develop the habit of doing what is right regardless of your audience and you will have an authentic lifestyle. As such, your source of happiness will be independent of uncontrollable factors. Why should you tie your happiness to someone else capable of ruining your day in a snap? This is not to mean that you will not need other people. Humans are social beings and interdependent. Letting them strongly influence your lifestyle is the major problem. Be your own man.

3. They Are Bold.

Boldly and cautiously pursuing their ambitions is part of the ingredients that make up happy people. Knowing what you want is one thing and pursuing it is another. If music is your passion and it makes you happy, chase after it for it is therein that your happiness lies. Whatever it is (of course considering its legality) do not let it pass.

To be truly happy, do not live in the shadow of other happy people. Define your happiness and drink from your well. Timidity will make you bask under the shade of giants and create a sense of false security. One day the shade will be no more and leave you exposed to an unimaginable reality.

4. They are social people.

Being social is one common characteristic of happy people. Happiness makes them bubbly and alive. There is a common testament in almost all happy people – either happiness made them social or their social nature made them happy. Thanks to whichever of the two came earlier, they are happy people!

Like bad luck, happiness is contagious. Your social circle can infect you with happiness or even deny it to you. Being sociable does not mean to the extreme nature with all the hype that comes along.

It means being approachable to people. Some will positively add to your basket and others will offer positive criticism towards your cause. With such input, your happiness will have longevity.

5. Believe in a greater cause.

Happy people understand that it is not always about them. There is a greater cause above their interests. They do not derive their happiness from the satisfaction of their needs and wants. Regardless of any deficiency in their lives, their flame of happiness is not easily put out.

Do you want to be happy? It is time to put self-interest aside and not tie your happiness to local anchors. An average person's happiness is mainly dependent on his well-being. Refusing to be average gives you leverage over those out to put off your happiness.

6. Lead a purposeful life.

Are there happy people without purpose? Those we see happy maintain their status by having a powerful drive towards the same. A strong purpose will make you stay on happiness' lane. It is the habit of happy people to have a purpose. This is to enable them to stay on course.

Being happy is not a permanent state. It is easily reversible if caution is not taken. Purposefulness is part of the caution taken by happy people.

7. Admit they are human.

To err is human. Given this, happy people appreciate the erroneous nature of man and accept the things they cannot change, have the courage to change the things they can, and the wisdom to know the difference. A prayer commonly referred to as the serenity prayer.

Admitting being human is the first step towards being happy. You forgive yourself of your wrongs before seeking the forgiveness of another. This brings inner peace culminating in happiness.

8. Know their strengths and weaknesses.

Being aware of your strengths and weaknesses is one thing happy people have mastered. Through that, they know their limits; the time to push and time to take a break. This serves to help avoid unwarranted disappointments that come along with new challenges.

Nothing can put off the charisma of a prepared spirit. Happy people know their limitations well enough such that no ill-willed voice can whisper disappointments to them. They hold the power of self-awareness within their hearts making them live with contentment.

9. Notice the contributions of those around them.

No man is an island. The contributions of other people in our lives cannot be emphasized enough. We are because they are (for all the good reasons). At any one point in our lives, someone made us happy. The first step is noticing the roles played by those in our immediate environment.

The joy of being surrounded by people to hold our hands in life is engraved deeper in our hearts in times of need. It is time you stop looking far away and turn your eyes to see what is next to you.

10. They are grateful and appreciative.

"Thank you" is a word that does not depart from the lips of happy people. Their hearts are trained to focus on what is at their disposal instead of what they cannot reach. It is crystal that a bird in hand is worth two in the bush.

Happy people continue being happy despite deficiencies. Try being appreciative and see how happiness will tow along.

Adopt these 10 habits of happy people and depression will keep away from you. If you want to be happy, do what happy people do and you will see the difference.

Chapter 17:

<u>10 Habits of Taylor Swift</u>

Well-versed pop star isn't the only description for the "American Sweetheart" Taylor Swift- She's a woman with many talents and abilities. As a world-famous singer-songwriter, accomplished businesswoman, and fitness guru, Swift has risen to become one of the world's most renowned celebrities.

She signed her first record deal at the age of 15, has been nominated for over 500 awards, has won 324, and has sold over 50 million albums. Such success did not simply land to her automatically. As per the new Netflix documentary Miss Americana, Swift's growth is a journey of countless disappointing and challenging life and career lessons.

Here are 10 habits of Taylor Swift that can enrich your life and career path.

1. Certainty

Getting to where you want to be in life credits a clear vision. With a sense of clarity, you can pave the way to reach that destination.

Since the day she started her career in music, Taylor Swift has been clear on what she wanted. From the very young age she has served to steer her decision making, and enjoyed every bit of it.

2. Focus on the Brighter Side

Taylor Swift has had a share of public scandals, tabloids exploitation, and people who aimed at tarnishing her name with controversy. It is irrelevant whether they are justified or not, she continues to produce and thrive in her positive space. Just like Taylor Swift, develop an urge to always working past the ruins while strengthening your optimistic moods.

3. You Have No Control Over What Happens

The incident at 2009 VMAs with Kanye West fuelled Swift's desire to prove that her talent is undeniable. You'll learn from the Concert's footage performing her most critically acclaimed song, "All Too Well", that she's was not up to changing what people would eventually say about her but was only concerned with respecting her work ethic. Make your response to criticism a reflection of respect for your hustle!

4. Credit Your Success to Having a Niche

In the entertainment business, and with successful people like Taylor Swift, each one has their unique niche/speciality that sets them apart from everyone else. Major deeply on what makes you unique and what brought you there as your storyline is only for you to tell.

5. Courage Is the Secret to Longevity

Taylor went from being a trial for sexual assault, which she won the case, to her mother ailing from breast cancer and brain tumour to all the publicized stunts she had been through. Despite the challenges, she managed to produce indisputably remarkable projects. Just like Taylor, your confidence, resilience, brilliance, work ethic, and steadfast trust in your process will definitely garner appreciation and respect.

6. Own Your Power

Taylor Swift not only has power, but she also owns it. Following Scooter Braun and Scott Borchetta incident, Taylor was not scared to jeopardize her image or face the consequences of speaking up against something she honestly believed was unfair.

There are always risks to speaking out, but sitting silence may be far riskier. In some circumstances, being silent may endanger your opportunity to manage a project or receive a promotion or increase.

7. Develop Your Support System

Nurture your relationships if you'd like to gain more influence. Even though you are not on the same scale as Taylor Swift, maintained friendships influences your world. Listen to them if you want them to listen to you.

8. Follow Your Heroes

Taylor Swift started her profession at a young age. Her childhood was fraught with difficulties but had motivation from her idols, whom she followed their advice. If you adore someone who influences your life path, emulating two or three things from them pays off.

9. Be Influential

Taylor's success in the music industry has been her driving force in influencing other people. You don't have to have her numbers to be impactful. When you devote your time and energy to becoming productive, influential stats and metrics will follow you.

10. Maintain a Healthy Lifestyle

Being a celebrity doesn't mean that Swift's healthy lifestyle is about trendy diets and strange eating habits that dominates the entire Hollywood culture. According to PopSugar, Swift eats salads, nutritious sandwiches, yoghurt and hit the gym regularly during the week.

Conclusion

You don't have to be Taylor Swift, but you can learn from her. Increase your influence, cultivate your network, develop credibility, wield your authority, focus on positivity, resilience is vital, and feel free to stand your ground as you work on your uniqueness.

Chapter 18:

Don't Stay At Home

Today we're going to talk about why you should consider getting out of your house as much as possible, especially if you need to get work done, or if you have some other important personal projects that requires your undivided attention to complete.

For those that work full-time jobs, we all aspire to one day be able to work from home. We all dream of one day being able to just get up from our beds and walk over to our desks to begin work.

Having tried this myself for the last 4 years, I can safely tell you that staying at home isn't all that amazing as it has been talked up or hyped up to be.

While it may sound nice to be able to work from home, in reality, distractions are tough to avoid, and procrastination is one major killer of productivity at home. Many of us have made our homes the Center of entertainment and relaxation. We buy nice couches, TVs, beds, speakers, etc, and all these items around the house are temptations for us to slack off.

For those who are living with family, or who have pets, their presence could also disrupt our productivity.

Without people around us to motivate us to keep working hard, we tend to just tell ourselves "it's okay I'll just watch this one show and then I'll get back to work", and before we know it, it is 5pm and we haven't done a single thing.

Some people love it, some people hate it, but personally, I much prefer getting my butt out of the house and into a co-working space, a cafe, or a library, where I can visually see other people working hard, which motivates me to stay away from slacking off.

Having been doing regular journaling to measure my productivity, staying at home has always resulted in my worst daily performance no matter how hard I try to make my home environment the most conducive for work. Feeling like taking nap because my bed is right there, or watching a Netflix show on my big screen tv, has always been hard to resist. You will be surprised how many hours you are potentially losing from just indulging in any of these things.

For those who really has no choice but to work from home, either to save money, or because you need to take care of a family member. I would highly suggest that you optimise your environment to give yourself the greatest chance of success.

Dedicate a room that will be made into your study/work room, ensure that there is adequate and bright lighting, and to Keep all possible distractions outside the room. Putting your work desk in your bedroom is the worst thing you can do because you will blur the lines between rest and work if you mix the two things up in one tiny space. Not only will you feel sluggish working from your bedroom, but you might also develop sleep issues as well.

Not staying at home is still your best bet for success. Find a space outside where you can be focused and have the discipline to get yourself there every single day, no matter how tired or lethargic you feel. Once you leave the house, you have already won half the battle in getting your productivity under control.

Chapter 19:

10 Habits of Millionaires

Millionaires are people who own quite a substantial amount of wealth. They have passed both the hundreds and thousands threshold and are moving towards the billion mark. They have common habits that a majority of them subscribe to.

Here are ten habits of millionaires:

1. They Are Ever Busy

Millionaires have upgraded from the thousands category over quite some time during which they worked day and night to increase their wealth portfolio. This has made them learn to be busy for a better part of their life.

They are busy strategizing on how they can make it to the next level and they do not have the luxury to relax. They are in a constant race against time and how they can make their businesses do better.

2. They Prioritize the Management of Their Property

Millionaires have vast wealth ranging from commercial and residential houses, vehicles, and land among other properties. They need to be extra vigilant on how they manage all their assets lest they lose them.

Sometimes they need to hire professionals to help them in management. Millionaires prioritize this because their property is their fortress and source of financial muscle. Moreover, they have a legal counsel to guide them not to transgress the law.

3. They Have A Diversified Investment Portfolio

Millionaires have invested heavily in every sector of the economy. They diversify their investment to cushion them from economic shocks like the one that gripped global economies during the coronavirus pandemic. This habit has made millionaires stay afloat despite economic depressions. It is a survival mechanism that you need to adapt if you also want to be a millionaire. Regardless of how better one economic sector performs, do not over-invest in it.

4. They Are Risk-Takers

Like gamblers, millionaires are risk-takers. Their risk appetite is insatiable. It is very difficult to talk them out of it. They can stake a portion of their investment and be ready to win it all or lose it all. Sometimes this habit pays off and that is what distinguishes them from common people. However, millionaires curb their risk appetite by seeking the advice of risk managers. They are advised whether or not an investment is viable before they commit to it. You should make calculated risk moves if you want a financial breakthrough. This is the lifestyle of millionaires.

5. They Are Hardworking

How do you think millionaires got there in the first place? It is through hard work and a lot of sacrifices. They have had to endure early mornings and late nights for them to achieve their current successes. It is not an easy journey to embark on.

Hard work sets them apart from those who want to reap in fields they have not planted. It is only fair for millionaires to harvest the fruits of their hard work. Begin working hard tirelessly until your efforts bear fruits.

6. They Are Disciplined

Hard work propels you to the top but discipline will maintain you there. Millionaires are disciplined in the use of their resources. They can account for every coin they spend. Such a level of financial discipline is rare and difficult to come by. This is what makes them stand out.

When you lead a disciplined life, you do not engage in activities that endanger your growth. The reason why millionaires grow while common people maintain the status quo is because the former are disciplined, unlike the latter who are easily tossed to and fro. Discipline is the key to seal your success.

7. They Verify Facts

Quite a few people would go a step further to verify what they are told. Millionaires do not take information at face value. They take the trouble to check the authenticity of their sources of information. It can be very disastrous if they act on heresy.

The businesses of millionaires could collapse if the public see its directors as untrustworthy. Gossip, rumors, and heresy do not build empires.

Maintain an unassailable reputation like millionaires if you want to grow like them.

8. They Have Thick Skin

Millionaires have risen to who they are because they did not listen to every voice that talked to them. They were sometimes talked out of decisions they made but they did not give in. At other times they were insulted by people they least expected but they remained steadfast.

You need to develop a thick skin like millionaires if you want to progress. Critics should not have the power to shout you to silence. Be like millionaires who will overlook the negativity of their critics and rise above their resistance.

9. They Are United

Millionaires are very united in their circles. They maintain close fellowship with fellow millionaires and never hesitate to come through for one another during hard times. This type of unity is rare in common people.

The unity of millionaires is to be emulated. This habit makes them stand out in society. United we stand, divided we fall. In their unity, millionaires protect their interests. In the absence of unity, they would all wither away like petals of a flower.

10. They Practice Corporate Social Responsibility

In the spirit of giving back to society, millionaires do corporate social responsibility in many ways. Through their companies and foundations, they build schools and hospitals for the community. It is how they express their gratitude to society.

There are tens, even hundreds of beneficiaries of acts of charity from millionaires. This has made it difficult for society to turn against millionaires because they also benefit from their businesses.

In conclusion, millionaires have these ten habits that distinguish them from others. Develop them slowly and watch yourself fit in their shoes.

Chapter 20:

7 Ways To Identify Your Weaknesses.

We find ourselves asking this question perhaps a million times, "What am I good at?" and a question that follows right after that, "What am I not good at?" The list of the latter is much longer. We can't entirely blame ourselves for thinking that we have more weaknesses than strengths. Our cultures and society are too focused on the notion that we should overcome our deficits and weaknesses rather than appreciating and emphasizing our efforts and strengths.

While it is true that there are some people who are naturally talented and possess a high degree of willpower that surpasses those who make little to no effort, it is also true that a person can improve, or at least try to improve his shortcomings to his maximum level of potential.

Here are 7 ways to help you identify your weakness and tackle them properly.

1. Appreciate yourself.

The first and foremost thing to do is to give yourself a round of applause and pat yourself in the back. You have kept your ego aside and actually started taking action because deep down, you know that you suffer from some weaknesses too, and you are willing to improve them. It takes so many guts to admit to yourself this and to sit down and work on yourself. You are already a strong person. Way to go!

2. Analyze your daily routine.

From the minute you wake up to the minute you lay down and close your eyes, observe everything that you do in the day. Recall that whether you did something productive or wasted your whole day. See if you procrastinated your way out of the critical tasks that were assigned to you, or you simply called in a lazy day hoping that you would either start your work late or will do it tomorrow. Perceive your relationships too, what things are you lacking that's distancing you from your loved ones. Once you've listed out all of your problems, it's time to re-evaluate yourself.

3. Check whether you have a negative mindset

As we are programmed to consume negativity first, we tend to notice our faults and flaws and the people's weaknesses first. We become thoroughly convinced that no matter how hard we will try, there's always someone better out there who will do this job effortlessly. But this is an inaccurate approach as we should challenge ourselves, recognize our weaknesses, see where we are lacking, and then try to change ourselves for the better. The best method to identify our weaknesses is through self-evaluation. But sometimes, we do need a helping hand to advise us and assist us in improving our weaknesses.

4. You Doubt Yourself

After convincing yourself that you lack hard work and dedication in some specific areas, I.e., you're not giving priority to your dreams and goals, you're making excuses not to make any efforts, you're giving too much or too little of yourself in your personal relationships; this activity is taking a considerable amount of my energy, I don't feel optimistic about doing this work, there's always someone better out there who will excel me, I'll get it done, but I need more time for it. I'll sacrifice my happiness for someone else, and I won't say the things that are bothering me; I don't care enough to put up with their moods. So you find yourself making senseless excuses just to avoid doing your share of work.

5. Find Out What Is Holding You Back

It is time for you to find out what exactly is it that you're suffering with. Is it a lack of time? Procrastination? Boredom? Selflessness? Selfishness? You might be surprised to know that it's none of the above. Instead, we create these situations in our minds to help us cope with our wasted time and not feel guilty about our actions (victim-blaming). The only reason that you might be suffering from is laziness or maybe low self-worth. You automatically assume that since everyone is doing better than you, you don't need to improve yourself or save your energy on doing the tasks you have no interest in. You're draining out too much of your energy dealing with your personal life that it's now reflecting on your mental health too, and all in all, you have started considering yourself weak and vulnerable. You feel as if you're failing at life, and nothing makes you feel better.

6. Start acknowledging your weaknesses.

We are well aware of the fact that nobody's perfect. In fact, an ideal person is the one who knows that he is full of flaws and doesn't try to hide them, takes any criticism positively, and works hard to improve himself. A person who doesn't admit to his mistakes and weaknesses will end up alone and unsuccessful. It is best to know that all people have downfalls and to acknowledge them. One should self-evaluate as well as discuss with some closed ones about his shortcomings. For example, some people might say that you get furious very quickly and on petty things; that is one quality you wouldn't be aware of as such. Or maybe if you sit in a quiet, dark room and relive your life experiences, you might end up seeing a pattern of mistakes that you make every time.

7. Challenge Yourself

These mistakes might be the reason that you're not yet where you want to be in your life. Give yourself challenging and struggling situations, and find solutions on how you would deal with them. Identify your areas of growth. See where you can make improvements. Sometimes, a particular activity or a particular relationship, or even a specific goal just isn't right for you, no matter how hard you try. Accept the fact with a big heart and open arms. Don't let yourself down, and start working on the areas you can improve by dedication, passion, and hard work. Observe if you are actually making yourself better through your actions, or you're just only using words. As action speaks louder than words, make sure your efforts are improving your weaknesses.

Conclusion:

We're more resilient than we give ourselves credit for. While it's undeniable that we all have weaknesses, and it takes a lot of nerve to admit to them, it's also true that one must accept them wholeheartedly and try to work towards betterment. Remember when you faced a strenuous situation, you felt like giving up because you felt so weak both physically and emotionally. But you rose from the ashes and got yourself out. Similarly, these weaknesses will try to bring us down at every step of our lives; we just have to make sure we don't succumb to them and keep our heads high. There's always room for improving ourselves and not to make our weaknesses and vulnerability get the best of us.

Chapter 21:

7 Reasons Your beliefs Are Holding You Back

You know that you have immense potential in your heart, and you are also working hard to attain your desired results, but something still doesn't fit right. Your beliefs might be consciously or unconsciously sabotaging your potential through your actions. This might create the less-than-desirable results that are holding you back from your real success.

Here are some 5 beliefs that might be getting in your way. Observe and analyze them, and start getting rid of them so that your path to success becomes easy and thorn-free.

1. Beliefs Are More Powerful Than You Think

"Beliefs have the power to create and the power to destroy. Human beings have the awesome ability to take any experience of their lives and create a meaning that disempowers them or one that can literally save their lives." - Tony Robbins. To change our lives, we first have to change our mindset and what we believe in so dearly. Challenging your beliefs is the key element to improve yourself. If we look around us, we might find a few limiting beliefs in the blink of an eye.

2. Everyone will get ahead of me if I rest.

This is perhaps the most crucial limiting belief that the majority of people go through. Many of us think that if we take some time off for ourselves, we'll fall behind in life, and everyone will get ahead of us, crushing us beneath them. For this particular reason, we stop focusing on our needs and necessities and burns out all of our energy on things that should come as second on our lists. Instead, we should convert our "shoulds" into "musts" and focus on ourselves too. Meditating for an hour, going to the gym, taking some time off for hanging out with friends or watching a movie alone, reading a book that's not connected to your work, these all are necessary to sustain life. Making excuses for not taking any time off for yourself and working day and night tirelessly will drain your energy or become a problem for your health; likewise, you will be tired physically and mentally and wouldn't be able to do your tasks on time.

3. Everyone is succeeding in life but me.

With the increasing social media norms and the lives of celebrities on every cover page, or seeing everyone around you figuring their lives out and enjoying themselves, you might feel that you are the only one who hasn't got a thing right. Unfortunately, human nature shows the world our successes and happiness rather than telling them our weak, struggling phases and vulnerability. Comparing yourself to those around you or any celebrity or influencer from social media may become a downward spiral for you when you are feeling confused and lost. Believing that everyone has it easy and you are the only one struggling could make you feel demotivated and depressed. This would, in turn, make you lazy, and you would eventually stop working towards your goal and passion.

4. I can never be good enough.

This limiting belief is the most common one among the people. Initially, they would give their all to a new job, a new relationship, or a new task. Then, if things wouldn't work out for them, they would just blame their performance and themselves and would label it as "I'm not good enough for this." This often leads to being anxious and finding perfection in things. And if failed to achieve this, one starts to procrastinate, thinking that their energies and efforts will eventually go to waste anyway. The little voice inside your head telling you that you're not good enough might also make you believe that you're not skilled enough or talented enough for the job or not deserving enough to be with the person you like. As a result, you pull yourself back and miss out on any opportunities offered to you.

5. I am capable enough to do everything myself.

We're often fooled by the idea that we don't need anyone's help, and we can figure out everything independently. This approach is majorly toxic as we all need a helping hand now and then. No one walks on the path of success alone. You may feel ashamed or guilty in asking for help or may think that you will be rejected or let down, or may think of yourself as the superior creature who knows everything and are not ready to listen to anyone else. All this might bring you down at one point in your life. We should always be open to any criticism and feedback and should never shy away from asking any help or advice from the people we trust and from the people we get inspired from.

6. The tiny voice becomes too loud sometimes

Limiting beliefs does impede us in some way. There's always this tiny voice in the back of our heads that keeps whispering thoughts and ideas into our minds. Most of what the voice tells us are negative stuff, and the worst part is that we actually start to believe in all of that. "You can never lose weight; stop trying. You're unattractive, and you won't find your significant other any time soon. You don't have the mindset or money to start up your own business; get yourself a 9-5 job instead." All of these, and much more, are what pulls us back from the things that we want to say or the stuff that we want to do.

7. The time isn't right.

The time isn't right, and believe me, it never will be. You're wasting your life away thinking that you will get married, lose your weight, learn a new skill, start your own business, all when the time will be correct. But there's no such as the right time. You either start doing what you want or sit on the side-lines and watch someone else do it. The right time is here and now. It would be best if you started doing the things you want until you make up your mind that you want to do it. You don't have to wait for a considerable amount of money to start a business; start with a small one instead. You don't have to settle down first to get married; find someone who will grow with you and help you. You don't need to spend hours and hours in the gym to lose weight; start eating healthy. There is no right time for anything, but the time becomes right when you decide to change yourself and your life for the better.

Conclusion:

You can make a thousand excuses or find a million experiences to back up your beliefs, but truth be told, you should always be aware of the assumptions you are creating and how they may be affecting your life. For example, will your beliefs stop you from taking action towards your life? Or will you change them into new and creative opportunities to get the results you want?

Chapter 22:

10 Habits That Make You More Attractive

Being attractive does not necessarily connote physical appearance. More than the physical appearance, attraction renders the mental, emotional, and spiritual energy irresistible to others. Some people radiate with their energy and confidence regardless of whether they have money, looks, or are socially connected. These people are just irresistible, and you will find that people will always approach them for advice, help, or even long-term companionships. What makes them more attractive? Their sense of self-worth is always from within their souls as contrasted with how they look from outside. They don't seek validation from others- but find it within themselves.

However, this is not genetically connected, but a habit that we can build within ourselves. You need to pursue and maintain such habits for the benefit of a greater you.

Here are 10 habits that make you more attractive:

1. Connect With People More Deeply.

Attractive people are always likable people, and being likable is a skill. Being likable means that you should be interested in hearing others out rather than spending all the time thinking and talking about yourself. As entrepreneur Jim Rohn puts it- "Irresistible or likeable people possess an authentic personality that enables them to concentrate more on those around them." This requires that you are in most cases over yourself, meaning that you don't spend more time only thinking about yourself.

To have this habit going on in you, try to take conversations seriously. Put that phone down and listen! Learn what those around you are into - Ask questions, enquire about their dreams, fears, preferences, and views on life. Focus on what is being said rather than what the response is or what impact that might have on you. Always aim to make others everyone feel valued and important.

2. **Treat Everyone With Respect.**

Being polite and unfailingly respectful is the key to being likable. If you are always rude to others, you will find that over time people will tend to avoid you. You should strive to not only be respectful to someone you know and like, but also to strangers that you come across with. Attractive people treat everyone with the same respect they deserve bearing in mind that no one is better.

3. **Follow the Platinum Rule.**

The commonly known version of the golden rule is that you should treat others the same way you want them to treat you. This comes with a major flaw: the assumption that everyone aspires to be treated similarly. The rule ignores the fact people are different and are motivated differently. For instance, one person's love for public attention is another's person's execrate. However, you can opt for this flaw by adopting the platinum rule instead. The notion is that you should only treat others as they want to be treated. Attractive people are good at reading others and quickly adjust to their style and behavior, and as a result, they can treat them in a way that makes them feel comfortable.

4. **Don't Try Too Hard To Put an Impression.**

Attractive people who are easily likable don't try too hard to impress. Liking someone comes naturally, and it depends on their personality. Hence if you spend most of the time bragging about your success or smartness, you are simply harming yourself without knowing it. People who try too hard to be liked are not likable at all. Instead they come across as narcissistic and arrogant. If you wish to be an attractive person choose to be humble and down-to-earth instead. People will see your worth with their own two eyes.

5. **Forgive and Learn From Your Mistakes.**

Learning from our mistakes is synonymous with self-improvement. It is proven that psychological traits are essential in human mating or relationships, meaning that both intelligence and kindness are key. Being intelligent, in this case, doesn't necessarily mean the PHDs or Degrees.

It means that a person can demonstrate intelligence by learning from mistakes they make and handling the same well. You demonstrate this also by being kind to yourself whenever you make a mistake and avoiding the same mistake in the future. Attractive people know how to not take themselves too seriously and to have a laugh at themselves once in a while.

6. Smile Often

People tend to bond unconsciously with the body language portrayed while conversing. If you are geared towards making people more attracted to you, smile at them when conversing or talking to them. A smile makes other people feel comfortable in conversations, and in turn, they do the same to you. The feeling is remarkably good!

7. Likable People Are Authentic and Are Persons of Integrity

People are highly attractive to realness. Attractive people portray who they are. Nobody has to expend energy or brainpower guessing their objective or predicting what they'll do next. They do this because they understand that no one likes a fake. People will gravitate toward you if you are genuine because it is easy to rely on you. On the flip side, it is also easy to resist getting close to someone if you don't know who they really are or how they actually feel.

People with high integrity are desirable because they walk their talk. Integrity is a straightforward idea, but it isn't easy to put into action. To show honesty every day, attractive people follow through with this trait. They refrain from gossiping about others and they do the right thing even if it hurts them to do so.

8. Recognize and Differentiate Facts and Opinions

Attractive people can deal gracefully and equally with divisive subjects and touchy issues. They don't shy away from expressing their views, but they clarify that they are just that: opinions, not facts. So, whenever you in a heated discussion, be it on politics or other areas with your peers, it is important to understand that people are different and are just as intelligent as you are. Everyone holds a different opinion; while facts always remain facts. Do not confuse the two to be the same.

9. Take Great Pleasure in The Little Things

Choose joy and gratitude in every moment – No matter if you are feeling sad, fearful, or happy. People who appreciates life for its up and downs will always appear attractive to others. Choose to see life as amazing and carefully approach it with joy and gratitude – Spread positive vibes and attract others to you that are also positive in nature. View obstacles as temporary, not inescapable. Everyone has problems, but it is how you deal with it each day that is important here. Optimistic people will always come out on top.

10.Treating friendships with priority.

True friendships are a treasure. When you take your time and energy to nourish true friendships, you will naturally develop others skills necessary to sustain all forms of relationships in your life. People will always gravitate to a person who is genuinely friendly and caring. They want to be a part of this person's life because it brings them support and joy. Take these friendships with you to the distance.

Bonus Tip: Do Your Best to Look Good

There is a huge difference between presentation and vanity. An attractive person will always make efforts to look presentable to others. This is comparable to tidying up the house before you receive visitors - which is a sign of gratitude to others. Don't show up sloppily to meetups and parties; this will give others the impression that you don't care about how you look which may put off others from approaching you. Always try your best in every situation.

Conclusion: Bringing it all in

Attractive people don't get these habits simply floating over their beds. They have mastered those attractive characteristics and behaviors consciously or subconsciously - which anyone can easily adopt.

You have to think about other people more than you think about yourself, and you have to make others feel liked, appreciated, understood, and seen. Note, the more you concentrate on others, the more attractive you will appear and become without even trying.

Chapter 23:

8 Ways to Discover What's holding You Back From Achieving Your Visions

We all have dreams, and I have no questions; you have made attempts at seeking after your goals. Oh, as a general rule, life's battles get the better of you and keep you down. The pressure of everyday life, again and again, puts you down. Regardless of your determination, devotion, and want, alone, they are not enough.

Being here exhibits you are not able to settle for a mediocre life and hidden desires. To help you in your goal of seeking after your objectives, you must become acquainted with those things keeping you down. When you do, you will want to eliminate every single reason keeping you down.

1. Fear

The deep-rooted foe is very likely a critical factor in keeping many of you from seeking after your objectives. It prevents you from acting, making you scared of venturing out. Dread is the thing that keeps you down. Dread is one reason why we don't follow what we truly need throughout everyday life.

• Fear of disappointment

• Fear of dismissal

• Fear of mocking

• Fear of disappointment

Quit allowing your feelings of fear to keep you down!

2. Procrastination

Putting things off till the following week, one month from now, one year from now, and regularly forever. You're not exactly sure the thing you're hanging tight for, but rather when whatever it happens, you'll be prepared to start seeking after your objectives. Be that as it may, this day never comes. Your fantasy stays as just a fantasy. Putting things off can just keep you down.

Quit allowing your Procrastination to keep you down!

3. Justifications

Do you find yourself procrastinating and making excuses for why you can't start working toward your goals? Those that succeed in accomplishing their objectives can overcome obstacles. So many individuals make excuses for themselves, believing they can't achieve a better career, start their own business, or find their ideal lifemate.

• It isn't the correct time

• I am insufficient

 • I am too old/young

Don't allow your excuses to hold you back any longer!

4. Lack of Confidence

Lack of confidence in yourself or your ability to achieve your goals will inevitably hold you back. Our actions, or lack thereof, are influenced by what goes on in our subconscious mind. We have self-limiting and negative beliefs that may be preventing us from enjoying an extraordinary life.

Nothing will be able to stop you if you believe in yourself. Bringing your limiting beliefs into focus will help you achieve your objectives.

Don't let your lack of confidence keep you back!

5. There Isn't A Big Picture

Others refer to what I call a breakthrough goal as a BHAG - Big Hairy Audacious Goal. A goal is what you need to keep you motivated and drive you to achieve it every day. Start small and dream big. You'll need a strong enough passion to propel you forward. Your ambitions will not motivate you until you first dream big.

For your objectives to be beneficial to you, they must assist you in realizing your ambitions. Those lofty ambitions. Goals can only motivate you, help you stay focused, and help you make the adjustments you need to make, as well as provide you the fortitude to overcome difficulties as you chase your big-picture dreams if they matter to you.

Stop allowing your big picture to stifle your progress!

6. Inability To Concentrate

Your chances of success are slashed every moment you lose focus. When we spread our focus too thin, we dilute our effort and lose the ability to focus on the most significant tasks. When you're pulled in a lot of different directions and have a lot of conflicting priorities fighting for your attention, it's easy to lose track of what's important. Any attempts to achieve vital goals will be harmed as a result of this.

Stop allowing your lack of concentration to keep you back!

7. Failure to Make a Plan

Finally, if you don't have a strategy, it's easy to become lost along the route. Consider driving across the country without a map, say from London to Glasgow. While you have a rough route in mind, there are many lands to cover and a lot of false turns and dead ends to be avoided. You can get there with the help of a GPS. It plots your path and creates a plan for you. A plan provides you with the road map you need to reach your objectives. This is the process of determining what you need to accomplish to reach your objectives. This is where you put in the time and effort to write out a plan of the steps you need to follow, the resources you'll need, and the amount of time you'll need to invest.

Stop allowing the lack of a strategy holds you back!

8. Not Keeping Track of Your Progress and Making Necessary Modifications

Goals, by their very nature, take time to attain. Therefore it's critical to keep track of your progress. You won't know what's working and what's not if you don't get quick and actionable feedback. You won't be able to tell when to alter or when to keep doing what you're doing. Anyone who is continuously successful in accomplishing their goals also reviews their goals and progress regularly. Regularly reviewing your goals allows you to make early modifications to stay on track.

Stop allowing not reviewing and adjusting your progress to hold you back!

Chapter 24:

8 Tips to Become More Resilient

Resilience shows how well you can deal with the problems life throws at you and how you bounce back. It also means whether you maintain a positive outlook and cope with stress effectively or lose your cool. Although some people are naturally resilient, research shows that these behaviors can be learned. So, whether you are going through a tough time right now or you want to be prepared for the next step in your life, here are eight techniques you can focus on to become more resilient.

1. Find a Sense of Purpose

When you are going through a crisis or a tragedy, you must find a sense of purpose for yourself; this can play an important role in your recovery. This can mean getting involved in your community and participating in activities that are meaningful to you so every day you would have something to look forward to, and your mind wouldn't be focusing on the tragedy solely. You will be able to get through the day.

2. Believe in Your Abilities

When you have confidence in yourself that you can cope with the issues in your life, it will play an important role in resilience; once you become confident in your abilities, it will be easier for you to respond and deal with a crisis. Listen to the negative comments in your head, and once you do, you need to practice replacing them with positive comments like I'm good at my job, I can do this, I am a great friend/partner/parent.

3. Develop a Strong Social Network

It is very important to be surrounded by people you can talk to and confide in. When you have caring and supportive people around you during a crisis, they act as your protectors and make that time easier for you. When you are simply talking about your problems with a friend or a family member, it will, of course, not make your problem go away. Still, it allows you to share your feelings and get supportive feedback, and you might even be able to come up with possible solutions to your problems.

4. Embrace Change

An essential part of resilience is flexibility, and you can achieve that by learning how to be more adaptable. You'll be better equipped to respond to a life crisis when you know this. When a person is resilient, they use such events as opportunities to branch out in new directions. However, it is very likely for some individuals to get crushed by abrupt changes, but when it comes to resilient individuals, they adapt to changes and thrive.

5. Be Optimistic

It is difficult to stay optimistic when you are going through a dark period in your life, but an important part of resilience can maintain a hopeful outlook. What you are dealing with can be extremely difficult, but what will help you is maintaining a positive outlook about a brighter future. Now, positive thinking certainly does not mean that you ignore your problem to focus on the positive outcomes. This simply means understanding that setbacks don't always stay there and that you certainly have the skills and abilities to fight the challenges thrown at you.

6. Nurture Yourself

When you are under stress, it is easy not to take care of your needs. You can lose your appetite, ignore exercise, not get enough sleep. These are all very common reactions when you are stressed or are in a situation of crisis. That is why it is important to invest time in yourself, build yourself, and make time for activities you enjoy.

7. Develop Problem-Solving Skills

Research shows that when people are able to come up with solutions to a problem, it is easier for them to cope with problems compared to those who can not. So, whenever you encounter a new challenge, try making a list of potential ways you will be able to solve that problem. You can experiment with different strategies and eventually focus on developing a logical way to work through those problems. By practicing your problem-solving skills on a regular basis, you will be better prepared to cope when a serious challenge emerges.

8. Establish Goals

Crisis situations can be daunting, and they also seem insurmountable but resilient people can view these situations in a realistic way and set reasonable goals to deal with problems. So, when you are overwhelmed by a situation, take a step back and simply assess what is before you and then brainstorm possible solutions to that problem and then break them down into manageable steps.

Chapter 25:

Five Habits of Good Speech Delivery

Speech delivery is a hot topic amongst many people with opinions divided on what to or what not to do. Everyone has their struggle in speech delivery; some are shy, others are bold but lack the material content to deliver while another group cannot hold a coherent conversation altogether with strangers.

Here are five fundamental habits of good speech delivery:

1. Understand Your Audience

Whenever given the chance to address an audience, it is imperative to understand the demographic constitution of your audience. Their age, social and political class contributes heavily to how they will perceive your speech.

The manner one can deliver a speech to a graduation class at a university is entirely different from how the same speech can be given to entrepreneurs considering the mindset and life priorities of these two groups.

When you have a thorough understanding of your audience, your art of public speaking and speech delivery will improve because your audience will relate well.

2. Read The Mood and Setting of Your Audience

The diction and language of your speech are variables of the prevailing mood of the audience. How can you relate with them if you are blind to their present mood (excitement or somberness) or the setting (high or low temperatures)?

The wearer of a shoe knows where it pinches. As a speaker, you should be flexible to allow your audience to follow your speech in their most comfortable state. If the weather is hot, allow them to open windows and air ventilation. If they are in a bad mood, make them understand that you feel their plight.

Be the bigger person in the room and accommodate everyone. It will earn you respect and your speech will be well received.

3. Understand the Theme of The Speech

This is the core subject matter of the speech. Every speech aims to pass a specific message to its recipients. Under no circumstances should the theme be lost to any other interest. If it does, the speech would be meaningless and a waste of time.

The onus is upon the deliverer of the speech to stick to the theme and neither alter nor dilute the message therein. He/she should first understand it to be able to convey the same to the audience. The speaker should not have any malice or prejudice to any section of the audience. They should have clean hands.

It is paramount to understand that the audience is not ignorant of the theme of the speech. When you disappoint their expectations, you would have lost their participation and some of them may leave the meeting in progress. The chance to deliver a speech does not render the rest of the audience is inferior to the speaker.

4. Be Bold

Boldness is the courage to speak fearlessly without mincing your words. Bold speakers are rare to come by and when they do, their audience becomes thrilled by their exuberance of knowledge. The content of a speech could be great but when a coward delivers it, the theme is lost.

Boldness captures the attention of the audience. They expect the best from a bold speaker. The best orators of our time speak so powerfully that one cannot ignore them. The 44th president of the United States is a perfect example of how he boldly delivered his speeches and commanded respect across the globe.

A bold speaker does not bore his/her audience and they are more likely to remember a speech that they delivered compared to those of timid speakers. Fortune favors the bold.

5. Engage Your Audience

It is important to bring onboard your audience when you are delivering a speech. They will feel included and it will be more of a conversation than a talk down. When an audience actively participates in the delivery of a speech, it is more likely they will remember it.

As a speaker, maintain eye contact with the audience. This will create a connection with them and remove the notion that you are afraid of them. From time to time in your speech, rope them in to answer a relatable question. An audience expectant of engagement from its speaker will be more attentive.

A speech is not a monologue. It is an interaction between the speaker and his/her audience. When a speaker monopolizes a speech, it becomes boring and easily forgettable. It may further come out as a show-off rather than a genuine speech of a particular theme.

These are the five key habits if you want to maximize the delivery of your speech.

Chapter 26:

Visualise Your Success In Life

When you have a clear idea of what you want in life, it becomes easier to achieve somehow. When you visualize yourself doing something, you automatically tend to get the results better. You can imagine your success in your mind before you even reach it so that it gives you a sense of comfort. You get the confidence that you can do whatever you desire. You complete your task more quickly because you have already done it once in your mind before even starting it. It relaxes us so we can interpret the outcome. You dream about your goals and remind yourself almost every day what you genuinely want or need. You become goal-oriented just by imagining your outcomes and results. Your brain tends to provide you with every possible option of opportunity you can have by visualizing. By this, you can take your dreams and desire into the real world and achieve them by knowing the possible outcome already.

Everyone today wants their picture-perfect life. They are derived from working for it, and they even manage to achieve it sometimes. People love the success which they had already estimated to happen one day. They knew they would be successful because they not only worked for it but, they also visualized it in their brains. Everything eventually falls into place once you remind yourself of your goals constantly and sometimes write it into a few words. Writing your goals down helps you immensely. It is the idea of a constant reminder for you. So, now whenever you look on that paper or note, you find yourself recognizing your path towards success. That is one of the ways you could visualize yourself as a successful person in the coming era.

Another way to visualize your success is through private dialogue. One has to talk its way through success. It's a meaningful way to know your heart's content and what it is you are looking for in this whole dilemma. You can then easily interpret your thoughts into words. It becomes easier to tell people what you want. It is an essential factor to choose between something. Weighing your options, analyzing every detail, and you get your answer. It requires planning for every big event ahead and those to come. You ready yourself for such things beforehand so that you will know the result.

Every single goal of yours will count. So, we have to make sure that we give our attention to short-term goals and long-term goals. We have to take in the details, not leaving anything behind in the way or so. We have to make sure that everything we do is considered by ourselves first. Short-term goals are necessary for you to achieve small incomes, giving you a sense of pride. Long-term plans are more time-consuming, and it takes a lot of hard work and patience from a person. Visualizing a long-term goal might be a risk, something as big as a long-term achievement can have loads of different outcomes, and we may get distracted from our goal to become successful in life. But, visualizing does help you work correctly to get to know what will be your next step. You can make schemes in your mind about specific projects and how to work them out. Those scheming will help you in your present and future. So, it is essential to look at every small detail and imagine short-term goals and long-term goals.

Visualizing your success creates creative ideas in your mind. Your mind gets used to imagining things like these, and it automatically processes the whole plan in your mind. You then start to get more ideas and opportunities in life. You just need to close your eyes and imagine whatever you need to in as vivid detail as possible. Almost everything done by you is a result of thoughts of your mind. It is like another person living inside of you, who tells you what to do. It asks you to be alert and move. It also means the result of the possible outcome of a situation. Every action of you is your mind. Every word you speak is your mind talking.

Chapter 27:

Top Life regrets of Dying Hospital Patients

The most common regret of dying people is

"I wish I'd had the courage to live a life true to myself, not the life others expected of me."

Why is this such a common dying regret at the end of our lives? And how can you make sure that you don't end up feeling the same way?

How to Be Courageous and Avoid the Biggest Regret

If you're reading this, then you probably have the power to make decisions in your daily life. Rarely, we are forced to live in a way that we don't want to live (thankfully). But somehow, many of us still end up wishing we had lived in a more true way to ourselves.

Here's why I believe this happens:

Anytime I find myself feeling stuck in neutral, it's usually the result of not having a clear target. I find myself doing work without defining what the work should be or hoping for a change without determining the underlying actions that would lead to it. In other words, I'm not clear about what I care about and how I can get there—more on this in a moment.

Here's the result:

If you never draw a line in the sand and clarify what is important to you, then you'll end up doing what's expected of you. When you don't have a clear purpose driving you forward, you default to doing what others approve of. We're not sure what we want, and so we do what we think other people want.

The gray areas in life usually arise when we haven't decided what we believe.

This is the position I think we all find ourselves in from time to time. And it's one reason why I think many of us end up living the life others expect us to live instead of a life that is true to ourselves.

I often think about how I can get better at living with purpose and live an important life instead of an urgent one. When it comes to being clear about what I'm doing and why I'm doing it, I like to use a technique that I call the Bullseye Method.

The Bullseye Method

"A skillful archer ought first to know the mark he aims at and then apply his hand, his bow, his string, his arrow, and his motion accordingly. Our counsels go astray because they are not rightly addressed and have no fixed end. No wind works for the man that has no intended post to sail towards."

— *Michel de Montaigne*

The quote above essentially says: "If you didn't know where the target was located, you would never fire an arrow and expect to hit the bullseye."

And yet, we often live our lives this way. We wake up and face the world day after day (we keep firing arrows), but we focus on everything *except* the bullseye.

For example, if you want to get in shape, then the bullseye is to become the type of person who never misses a workout. That's on target. And yet, many of us spend our time looking for a stronger bow (workout program) or a better arrow (diet plan), or a tighter string (running shoes). Those things matter, but none of them serve you if you're not firing arrows in the right direction.

The Bullseye Method ignores the things we typically focus on, like tactics, resources, or tools. Instead, it focuses on the identity and location of the bullseye. It forces us to be clear about what we want from life.

In other words, forget about how you want to perform or what you want to look like. A bullseye is not "gain 10 pounds of muscle" or "build a successful business." The bullseye is living a life that's on target. It's having a purpose and a clear direction for the actions you will take.

What type of person do you want to become? What type of values do you want to stand for? Which actions do you want to become your habits?

The only way to live a life that is true to you is to have a purpose of organizing your life around. Where is your bullseye located?

Chapter 28:

Why Are You Working So Hard

Your why,

your reason to get up in the morning,

the reason you act,

really is everything - for without it, there could be nothing.

Your why is the partner of your what,

that is what you want to achieve, your ultimate goal.

Your why will be what pushes you through the hard times on the path to your dreams.

It may be your children or a burning desire to help those less fortunate, whatever the reason may be,

it is important to keep that in mind when faced with troubles or distractions.

Knowing what you want to do, and why you are doing it,

is of imperative importance for your life.

The tragedy is that most people are aiming for nothing.

They couldn't tell you why they are working in a certain field even if they tried.

Apart from the obvious financial payment,

They have no clue why they are there.

Is financial survival alone really a good motive to act?

Or would financial prosperity be guaranteed if you pursued greater personal preference?

Whatever your ambitions or preference in life,

make sure your why is important enough to you to guarantee your persistence.

Sometimes when pursuing a burning desire,

we can become distracted from the reason we are working.

Your why should be reflected in everything you do.

Once you convince yourself that your reason is important enough, you will not stop.

Despite the hardships, despite the fear, despite the loss and pain.

As long as you maintain a steady path of faith and resilience,

your work will soon start to pay off.

A light will protrude from the darkness and the illusionary troubles sent to test your faith will disappear as if they were never here.

Your why must be strong.

Your what must be as clear as the day is to you now.

And your faith must be eternal and unwavering.

Only then will the doors be opened to you.

This dream can be real, and will be.

When it is clear in the mind with faith, the world will move to show you the way.

The way will be revealed piece by piece, requiring you to take action and do the required work to bring your dream into reality.

Your why is so incredibly important.
The bigger your why, the greater the urgency, and the quicker your action will be.

Take the leap of faith.
Do what you didn't even know you could.
Never mind anyone else.
Taking the unknown path.
Perhaps against the advice of your family and friend,
But you know what your heart wants.

You know that even though the path will be dangerous, the reward will be tremendous.
The risks of not never finding out is too great.
The risk of never knowing if you could have done better is unfathomable.
You can always do better, and you must.

Knowing what is best for you may prove to be the most important thing for you.
How you feel about the work you are doing,
How you feel about the life you are living,
And how do you make the most of the time you have on this earth.
These may prove far more important than financial reward could ever do for you.

Aim to strike a balance.

A balance between working on what you are passionate about and building a wealthy financial life.

If your why and will are strong enough,

Success is all but guaranteed for you – no second guesses needed.

Aim for the sky,

However high you make it,

you will have proven you can indeed fly.

Chapter 29:

6 Ways To Attract Anything You Want In Life

It is common human nature that one wants whatever one desires in life. People work their ways to get what they need or want. This manifestation of wanting to attract things is almost in every person around us. A human should be determined to work towards his goal or dreams through sheer hard work and will. You have to work towards it step by step because no matter what we try or do, we will always have to work for it in the end. So, it is imperative to work towards your goal and accept the fact that you can't achieve it without patience and dedication.

We have to start by improving ourselves day by day. A slight change a day can help us make a more considerable change for the future. We should feel the need to make ourselves better in every aspect. If we stay the way we are, tomorrow, we will be scared of even a minor change. We feel scared to let go of our comfort zone and laziness. That way, either we or our body can adapt to the changes that make you better, that makes you attract better.

1. **Start With Yourself First**

We all know that every person is responsible for his own life. That is why people try to make everything revolves around them. It's no secret that everyone wants to associate with successful, healthy, and charming people. But, what about ourselves? We should also work on ourselves to become the person others would admire. That is the type of person people love. He can also easily attract positive things to himself. It becomes easier to be content with your desires. We need to get ourselves together and let go of all the things we wouldn't like others doing.

2. Have A Clear Idea of Your Wants

Keeping in mind our goal is an easy way to attract it. Keep reminding yourself of all the pending achievements and all the dreams. It helps you work towards it, and it enables you to attract whatever you want. Make sure that you are aware of your intentions and make them count in your lives. You should always make sure to have a crystal-clear idea of your mindset, so you will automatically work towards it. It's the most basic principle to start attracting things to you.

3. Satisfaction With Your Achievements

It is hard to stop wanting what you once desired with your heart, but you should always be satisfied with anything you are getting. This way, when you attract more, you become happier. So, it is one of the steps to draw things, be thankful. Be thankful for what you are getting and what you haven't. Every action has a reason for itself. It doesn't mean just to let it be. Work for your goals but also acknowledge the ones already achieved by you in life. That way you will always be happy and satisfied.

4. Remove Limitations and Obstacles

We often limit ourselves during work. We have to know that there is no limit to working for what you want when it comes to working for what you want. You remove the obstacles that are climbing their way to your path. It doesn't mean to overdo yourselves, but only to check your capability. That is how much pressure you can handle and how far you can go in one go. If you put your boundaries overwork, you will always do the same amount, thus, never improving further. Push yourself a little more each time you work for the things you want in life.

5. Make Your Actions Count

We all know that visualizing whatever you want makes it easier to get. But we still cannot ignore the fact that it will not reach us unless we do some hard work and action. Our actions speak louder than words, and they speak louder than our thoughts. So, we have to make sure that our actions are built of our brain image. That is the way you could attract the things you want in life. Action is an essential rule for attracting anything you want in life.

6. Be Optimistic About Yourselves

Positivity is an essential factor when it comes to working towards your goals or dreams. When you learn to be optimistic about almost everything, you will notice that everything will make you satisfied. You will attract positive things and people. Negative vibes will leave you disappointed in yourself and everyone around you. So, you will have to practice positivity. It may not be easy at first while everyone around you is pushing you to negativity. That is where your test begins, and you have to prove yourself to them and yourself. And before you know it, you are attracting things you want.

Conclusion

Everyone around us wants to attract what they desire, but you have to start with yourself first. You only have to focus on yourself to achieve what you want. And attracting things will come naturally to you. Make sure you work for your dreams and goals with all your dedication and determination. With these few elements, you will be attracting anything you want.

Chapter 30:

If Today Was Your Last Day

If today was your last day, what would you do with your life? Steve Jobs once said that "For the past 33 years, I have looked in trhe mirror every morning and asked myself: '**If today** were the **last day** of my life, would I want to do what I am about to do **today**?' And whenever the answer has been 'No' for too many **days** in a row, I know I need to change something.".

Do you agree with that statement? For me I believe that it is true to a certain extent. I argue that not many of us have the luxury of doing what we love to do every single day. As much as we want to work at that dream job or earn that great salary, or whatever that ideal may be, for some of us who have to feed a family or make ends meet, it is just not possible. And we choose to make that sacrifice to work at a job that we may not like, or go through a routine that sometimes might seem a drag. But that's a personal choice that we choose to make and that is okay too.

On the flip side, i do believe that for those who have the luxury and the choice to pursue whatever careers, dreams, hobbies, and interests we want to pursue, that we should go for it and not live life in regret. I have heard of countless friends who work at a job they hate day in and day out, complaining about their life every single day and about how miserable they are, but are too afraid to leave that job in fear of not being able to find something they like or in fear that their dreams would not work out. Not because they couldn't afford to do so, but because they are afraid. This fear keeps them trapped in a never ending cycle of unhappiness and missed opportunities.

Personally, I'm in the camp of doing something you dislike even if u struggle with it if it can provide you with some financial security and pay your bills, whilst at the same time pursuing your dreams part time just to test the waters. You have the comfort of a monthly stream of income while also taking a leap of faith and going after what you really want to do in life. And who knows it could work out some day. In the present moment, I'm actually working on many different interests and hobbies. I do the necessary work that i hate but explore other areas that brings me joy, and that is what keeps be going. I have a passion for singing, songwriting, tennis, and making videos like this that not only educates but also aims to bring joy to others. My full-time job only fulfils my bank account while my interests and work that i do on the side fulfils my heart and soul. And who knows, if any one of these side hobbies turn out into something that I can make some money with, hey it's a win win situation now don't you think?

I challenge each and every one of you to go ahead and take a leap of faith. Time waits for no one and you never know when your last day might be. Koby Bryant died suddenly from a helicopter crash at a young age of 41. But I would argue that because he pursued his dreams at a young age, he has already lived a wonderful and fulfilling life as opposed to someone who is too afraid to do what they want and hasn't lived up to their fullest potential despite living until 90. You have also heard of Chadwick Boseman who was immortalised as a great human being who gave it his all despite fighting colon cancer. He pursued his dreams and I bet that he had no regrets that his life had to end earlier than it should. And to Steve jobs, he gave us Apple, the biggest company in the world by pursuing his dream of changing the world and the way we communicate with one another. Without him we wouldn't have all our favourite beloved apple products that we use today. Without him there might not be amazon, google, Facebook because there wouldn't be apps and there wouldn't be devices that people used to do all these things with.

But most importantly, this is about you. How do you want to live your life, and if today was your last day, what would you do differently and how would this carry on to all other areas of your life. Your relationships with your family, your relationship with your friends, your partner. And do you feel fulfilled as a human being or do you feel empty inside. It is never too late to turn your life around and make choices that will make your heart fill with immense joy and gratitude until your life truly ends. So make the decision right now to honour yourself by living your day to the fullest, coz you never know when it might be your last.